Save the Males

Changing Men . . . Changing the World

by

Tom Owen-Towle

Cover image: "Unbridled Spirit," by Tony Sheets

This painting is one of several I created to depict a dream I had after my father died in 1989. The dream included an epiphany with my father in which he set me free as an artist and a person. While he was alive he had been my mentor. We were both professional artists, though I had trained as a sculptor to avoid the obvious difficulty of working in the larger-than-life shadow of the noted American artist he was. He started me painting when I was in my mid-30s, saying that I had avoided being a painter long enough. We painted together in many parts of the world, but he always maintained the role of my teacher right up to the day he died.

"Unbridled Spirit" represents the part of the dream when Dad set me free, as an artist and as his son. He told me to create from what I felt with my own inner spirit and style. In this painting, I am the horse being unbridled from all the binds of human expectations, especially those of my father. I was now free to give and to create, the two greatest gifts for an artist. For me, Tom's book is about freedom, for only knowledge can truly set us free as men to give back to humankind.

—Tony Sheets, 2003

ISBN: 0-9702479-4-X

Editing, design, and layout by Laura Horton

Dedication

This book is a gift for our Unitarian Universalist grandsons and granddaughters—indeed, for all the little ones of the world, known and unknown—that they might have healthy male mentors around, as well as viable brothering paths, when they go hunting for them.

We would bequeath not merely some money or platitudes but a mighty movement of mature masculinity for the boys and girls coming after us.

Table of Contents

The Challenge
Ultimately, It's about Salvation!
"For the Whole World Are We Born"
Caring about Our Men . . . and Boys
Males Are Primary Carriers and Targets of Violence
Perverted Patriarchy Is a Culprit
Stopping Violence against Women and Children
Horizontal Violence Is Rampant
An Epidemic of Self-Violence
We Remain a Band of the Cautiously Hopeful
Following in Brother Jacob's Footsteps
"Tell Them about the Dream, Martin!"

Where Art Thou, Brother?
It's the Church's Job to Feed the Souls of Men
The WHAMMM Factor
Maturing from Boyhood to Brotherhood
A Painful Personal Passage

Caregivers: Power FOR
Collaborators: Power ALONGSIDE
Resisters and Reconcilers: Power AGAINST and ACROSS
Followers: Power UNDER
Epilogue

Our Demonic Male Legacy
Two Intertwining Truths
    Violence is Pervasive
    Violence Begets Violence
The Necessary Gift of Kindly Aggression
Healthy Male Aggression
Letter from a Minister to a Marine

Male Menopause Is Real
Eldering: Yesterday and Today
The Church Exists to Serve Its Gray-Heads
Ways to Honor Our Sages
Younger and Older Men Save Each Other
Men Blessing and Being Blessed
    Blessing
        Serving Others
        Taking Risks
        Grandfathering
    Being Blessed
        Souling
        Shedding
        Surrendering

Foreword

Save the Males is about universal salvation. It's a guidebook written for Unitarian Universalist men who want to walk their spiritual talk. Tom Owen-Towle calls this practice *compassionate brothering*. Each act transforms personal quest into pathways for the engaged heart.

My heart has been transformed by Tom's work throughout the years as brother, friend, and colleague. Tom calls all of us as brothers and sisters of the way. Universal salvation means men, too. None of us can be left behind.

Tom's own struggle for salvation informs his calling as minister, teacher and writer. His passion, his presence, and his radical attentiveness to men's stories shine from every story in this book. Tom knows that men heal one another into wholeness through the practice of wholehearted engagement, open-minded reflection, and personal commitment. As brothers and sisters who journey on this path of transformation together, we must pay attention to each other's stories.

We begin with our own stories. We must hear each other into being. *Save the Males* is filled with stories of men who experience religious transformation. These men are brothering each other into life anew, together. They do it. You can do it. We all must do it.

I call this book a life plan for beginners, a lesson plan for fellow sojourners, and a journal for spiritual masters. Think about how you act in the world, Tom says, and think about how you feel inside. Pay attention to your inner feelings. Practice compassionate understanding. Listen deeply to the soul stories of your sisters and brothers. Moment by moment, day by day, these practices create the space between you and another so that we can all meet in wholeness. Tell your stories again and again and you generate what we all need: saving grace. Together, brothers and sisters, we will change this world.

Through *Save the Males,* Tom draws our attention to the specifics of transformation. Read carefully. Read reflectively. Read passionately. Read prayerfully. Read with your brothers. Read with your sisters. Read beyond dogmatic claims that have injured us. Read beyond traditions that defy logic and reason. Read to affirm our inherent value. Read to sustain the worth and dignity of human nature. Read to freedom.

We know human salvation is not a solo act. That's why we travel together as brothers and sisters on this journey. Our brother Tom brings us on a sacred journey of self-discovery. Our brother Tom calls us to be open, honest and self-disclosing. Our brother Tom has extended his arm through *Save the Males.* Reach out and take it. Risk. Love. Live. Nobody can be left behind.

Thandeka
Associate Professor of Theology and Culture
Meadville Lombard Theological School

Preface

Save the Males started with six lectures delivered throughout 2002–2003 to Unitarian Universalists in the Chicago, Berkeley, and Boston areas. Understandably, I've made additions and corrections to convert this spoken project into a readable book. However, the passional tenor of the original presentations, delivered live from heart to heart, should resound from every page. These talks were followed by vigorous dialogue and often accompanied with tears on both sides of the podium.

I'm indebted to many folks, starting with the members of the Minns Committee (especially its able chair, the Rev. Jeffrey Barz-Snell) who boldly selected me to be the conveyor of this rather unusual, if not radical, topic. And to Susan Minns who launched this lectureship-dream in 1941, the very year I was born, I'm profoundly grateful for this chance to bare my masculine soul.

Additional thanks go to Bill Murry for graciously hosting the first two lectures, then inviting me to publish it under the Meadville Lombard Press imprint. Bill and Barbara Hamilton-Holway, Thomas Mikelson, and Stephen Kendrick were all staunch advocates of this project as well, kindly inviting me to present the lectures in their Unitarian Universalist households. And Laura Horton, one of our promising seminary students at Meadville Lombard Theological School, has done a superior job of preparing this volume for publication.

But it all goes back much further than this past year. The men of my Unitarian Universalist Men's Fellowship in San Diego have been my beloved buddies since 1978. And, in truth, my masculine pilgrimage started in 1973 when we launched the Men's Awareness Liberation Effort

(M.A.L.E.) in Pasadena, California. A holy remnant of that dauntless venture endures some 30 years later.

Changing men changes the world. I stake my life on that proposition. And so do countless other brothers in our liberal religious fold.

Tom Owen-Towle
June 2003
San Diego, California

Chapter 1: Ultimately, It's about Salvation

We, with love, shall force our brothers to see themselves as they are, to cease fleeing from reality and begin to change it.

—James Baldwin

The Challenge

There's been a massive withdrawal from participation in the life of American society in recent history. This was documented in Robert Putnam's trenchant book entitled *Bowling Alone: The Collapse and Revival of American Communities*, a volume that vividly portrays our society breaking down due to severe disconnection from families, neighborhoods, organizations, even the republic itself. *Bowling Alone* especially evidences a retreat of men from communal involvement in everything civic.

Furthermore, during the past 25 years, when the bulk of mainline churches and temples have lost millions of members, statistics show that more men than women have left. The numbers of men in attendance and leadership (both lay and professional) have been diminishing within Unitarian Universalism as well.

Speaking to the condition of our own faith-communion, I contend this exodus is primarily occurring because adult men comprise the least-nourished constituency in our liberal religious ranks. We are inadequately satisfying the deeper appetites of our men, whether voiced or unvoiced—hungers for a mature religious masculinity that will produce authentic soulful and prophetic growth, inner sustenance and outer purpose.

Although men may continue to transact business per usual, their interiors are aching for solace and direction. I know, and so do you, too many men leading "lives of quiet desperation," to quote forebrother Henry David Thoreau's ominous phrase.

I'm not recommending that we beat a hasty retreat from what has been, in recent decades, an essentially healthy feminization of our movement. Not at all. My partner in life and ministry, Carolyn, has embodied feminine reality at its fullest, and I've aspired to be her soulmate as an ardent, unabashed pro-feminist man. For better, for worse, forever.

Nourishing the health and holiness in both women and men are not oppositional, but mutually reinforcing, endeavors. Both are passional vows we must make and sustain as a progressive movement, lest we slither into irrelevance.

Decades ago, women gathered and said: "We need a women's federation. We must band together as women to accomplish what we can't do singly. Our organization will exist apart from but not against men!" Well, in the waning moments of the 20th century, some of us convened to launch a brothering path for men in alignment with Unitarian Universalist principles and directives. We named it the *Unitarian Universalist Men's Network*. That was a noble start, but we've got to keep on keeping on.

In this book I'm throwing down the gauntlet to our religious tradition. I'm exhorting us to pledge abundant resources to the intentional care and feeding of the mature masculine soul—simultaneously with continuing our dogged commitment to women. Unitarian Universalism must accompany men in the honorable yet rugged quest to become what the 13th-century Persian Sufi poet Rumi called "hunters of more invisible game."

When Robert Bly was asked, some years back, to establish a nationwide "men's movement," and to serve at its helm, he quickly retorted "that the last thing men need today is another political union with one of them as its boss, another king of the mountain; for what is truly happening to men is occurring inside men. It's essentially an interior revolution." But I would quickly amend: an interior revolution that produces significant behavioral adjustments as well. The brothering transformation I'm espousing will alter men in both soulful and prophetic ways.

A related note. When we launched UUMeN in 1993, its charge was to be a clearinghouse for exchange of information of special interest to Unitarian Universalist men and to work alongside other continental organizations committed to the same goals. But the emphasis was always indigenous: to help local Unitarian Universalist men and groups foster "a broad range of brothering communities that provide opportunities for growth in a trustworthy atmosphere."

Men have been well schooled in building continental empires and monolithic movements. The founding brothers of UUMeN agreed that we didn't need another centralized club but could better serve our own men by encouraging them to grow personally, socially, and spiritually in their home tribes. Men can all too readily avoid soul work, as well as prophetic service, merely by proliferating bureaucratic structures and conducting business meetings.

Our emphasis from the outset was to think globally and to act locally—to bid men to serve a vision beyond our own egos while still working the soil where we dwell. As Jean Houston puts it: "We overcome detachment and ineffectiveness by joining local life to great life." In the brothering path we seek to marry the unit and the universal.

Ultimately, It's about Salvation!

Since I began men's work 30 years ago, my bedrock premise hasn't altered much, indeed it's been fortified: changing men changes the world! And why do men need to change? For our very own good *and* for the well-being of all living entities that we touch. And it will be "change that comes out of foundation, not fireworks," to use a phrase from Gail Godwin's *Evensong*.

As an unrepentant missionary, I would further declare that if we Unitarian Universalists want a saner globe, more merciful homes, more equitable workplaces, more satisfying gender and racial bonds, then we will be emboldened to do the gloriously tough yet fulfilling work of occasioning a fresh, invigorated version of masculinity in Unitarian Universalism.

When men change—soulfully and prophetically, internally and externally—everyone will benefit. Moreover, the entire Creation will be mended. Men's beleaguered bodies and stunted souls will rebound. The majority of women and children will leap exuberantly. Violence of every sort will most assuredly diminish. Animals and plants will be seen to spring heavenward. Even the deities can be expected to throw a party.

I bet my life on that hope and try to behave accordingly.

Men's work spells nothing less and nothing more than transformation—I'll up the ante: salvation. This sentiment of changing men as a salvational venture first came home to me when I was ministering in Davenport, Iowa in the mid-1970s. A man I'll call Bill (his name, like the names of other men who appear in this book, has been changed) arrived in town, to set up his own dinner theater. Unfortunately, Bill never accomplished that dream during his time among us, but something else did happen. Bill's soul caught on fire.

He wrote songs for our church, led group discussions on Unitarian Universalism, played on our church softball team, and portrayed historical personages, Mark Twain and Benjamin Franklin being his specialties. But more than that, Bill was awakened from a spiritual slumber. As he was leaving our area to return to New England to rejoin his family—after his valiant experiment in America's heartland—Bill testified during a farewell worship service. He said something I've taken to heart ever since: "I entered this Unitarian outpost in order to receive some intellectual nourishment, maybe occasional enlightenment, but I got more: I was saved—saved from myself and saved for the world. Hallelujah, thanks be to you folks as well as to the Eternal Spirit!" "Saved" was Bill's exact word, and this, my friends, was 30 years ago when our movement never mentioned anything about saving or being saved, unless in the past tense and with derision.

I've seen such a salvational change happen, with my own eyes, to hundreds of men; yea, it's happened periodically to my own crusty, gnarled soul as well. I've seen men whose lives have turned outside-in (reflectively), then inside-out (prophetically) again—men who have become gentler yet stronger males at home. Men who have dared to quit their secure jobs, because the posts became too confining or incongruent

4

with their values. Men who have left all sorts of closets for closer encounters with life. Men who have dumped much fear for much love. Men who have marched for causes they wouldn't even write checks for in earlier days. Men, who have left unhealthy bonds, wobbled, whined, and wept for awhile, then stood tall and moved ahead. Men who have agonizingly matured, right in front of us, into a more suitable sexual orientation.

I've seen men massage men's backs; using their hands, for the first time, to touch another man for healing, not hurt. And, afterwards, pledging never to do harm with their own hands ever again . . . to anyone, anything. I've seen men, who've been emotionally constipated most of their lives, never stop crying for an entire weekend, their tears wetting, then cultivating, the very ground upon which they stand.

Can you feel the earth shake a bit and the heavens sing some when imagining such kinds of saving passages?

I've seen men finally "get" the ravaging reality of racism, often when unavoidably facing a burdensome condition of their own. I've seen men emerge from prison life to tell stories of agony in our safe, saving circles . . . then other men, converted by the confessions, stirred to go forth and work in brothering other men behind bars.

I could go on and on. And we will; we must never run out of opportunities for men—starting with the very ones in our own household—to bravely unravel sagas of bone-deep hurt and spirit-soaring hope in sacred circles that gladly harbor their hearts.

That's why we have our churches—that's why we need men's groups, to enable more and more men to become brothers—for that's how males are truly saved . . . brother by brother by brother.

I'm reminded of the fact that in our Universalist tradition members were expected to refer to each other as "brother" or "sister"; indeed, in the early years of American Universalism, the term "Reverend" was seldom used in reference to clergy. A male minister was a brother, your spiritual peer. The truth is that level glances and active gazes only come from genuine brothers and sisters, whether linked in faith or greeted on the road.

Brothering means choosing to relate respectfully and intimately, starting with yourself, branching out to other men, then connecting justly with women and children, and moving outward to form healthy kinship with all of creation. Brothering unquestionably marks a bold, evolutionary leap in the maturing of males!

"For the Whole World Are We Born"

Now, by talking about saving the males, I'm not trying to be precious or exclusionary. We've got to save the females, the whales, the males, and more. The whole universe—what Kurt Vonnegut calls "The Great Big Everything"! In truth, we Unitarian Universalists venture our lives on the conviction that all reality is utterly interconnected. So, saving one portion of existence banks on saving the rest of it.

There's a slogan that served as the family motto of Bishop John A. T. Robinson from Great Britain: *Non nobis solum sed toti mundo nati*, "Not for ourselves alone but for the whole world are we born." Another version, if you will, of our all-encompassing Unitarian Universalist theology.

But, like it or not, I arrived as a male being and have chosen to stay one, thereby fulfilling my genderal vocation. Accordingly, as a man, any momentous change must begin with my own incarnation and radiate forth from there. I can't afford to get stuck on myself, but I've got to begin there. Furthermore, when I say "save the males," I'm talking about *all* men, not just men I like or men who resemble my opinions, men dwelling in my homeland, men of a particular race, faith-choice or class, ability or orientation. No, I concur with Walt Whitman, who claimed that "all men are my brothers."

This clarion call for such a brothering revolution shouldn't come as a surprise. For aren't mosques, churches, temples, and sanghas commissioned to be centers of redemption? Aren't religious homes in business principally to strengthen the character of their adherents? Aren't tribes like ours supposed to be focused upon nothing less than full-blown repentance and renewal?

James Luther Adams, the premier Unitarian Universalist theologian of the 20th century, pinpoints the change-agent imperative of religious bodies in the following tale:

Some years ago I was a member of the Board of Trustees of the First Unitarian Church in Chicago. A member of the Board often complained about the minister preaching too many sermons on race relations. He often said that academics, of course, know little of the world of reality. One evening at a meeting of the Board he opened up again. So the question was put to him, "Do you want the minister to preach sermons that conform to what you've been saying about 'kikes' and 'blacks?'" "No," he replied, "I just want the church to be more realistic."

Then the barrage opened, "Will you tell us what's the purpose of a church anyway?" "I'm no theologian. I don't know." "But you have ideas, you're a member here, a member of the Board of Trustees, and you're helping to make decisions. Go ahead, tell us the purpose of the church. We can't go on unless we have some understanding of what we're up to here." The questioning continued, and items on the agenda for the evening were ignored.

At about one o'clock in the morning our friend became so fatigued that the Holy Spirit took charge. And he gave a remarkable statement regarding the nature of our fellowship. Our friend said, "The purpose of the church is . . . well, the purpose is to get hold of people like me and change them!"

So it is. The job of our liberating religion is, frankly, to convert us—literally to turn us around toward healthier, happier, and holier lives as earthlings. That includes saving the males: from themselves and for themselves. More than that, saving males from harming others and for reforming society and respecting the planet.

But, alas, religious communities fall short of being stimulating, let alone salvational, centers of change—Unitarian Universalists societies included. Instead religion too often produces reinforcers of the status quo rather than movers and shakers. Granted, individual Unitarian

Universalists challenge the gender stereotypes and injustices prevalent in modern society. And we possess congregations that create kinship circles supporting men to become more soulfully alive and prophetically responsive. But the numbers are modest.

Caring about Our Men . . . and Boys

Men's attendance is down in our churches: by some estimates, only one man for every two women. Numbers of men being attracted to professional religious leadership are flagging. And, if truth be told, most men, in local congregations of any stripe or size, are still lodged in traditional roles of doing maintenance work, raising the funds, and leading boards. Men as religious educators, paid or volunteer, are the exception. Fostering viable boy-friendly programming remains a live challenge for most of our parishes.

The numbers of Unitarian Universalist societies that exhibit a men's table on their premises, let alone sustain a continuous brothering path, are few and far between. And some groups have been known to piddle out after an initial burst of energy. An annual Father's Day service, infrequent potluck-discussions, or even a five-week series won't suffice; they constitute mere blips on any local ecclesiastical screen.

There are plenty of explanations but no good excuses for the glaring dearth of steady programming to assist men in their arduous (yet playful) work on the road toward becoming more mature liberal religious pilgrims. We must do better by and for our men. Remember: one raison d'être of sanghas, churches, temples, and mosques is to save the males!

There must be specific male-based growth options available on every Unitarian Universalist church campus, otherwise men will continue to show up in modest numbers, fade away from deeper involvement, or only participate in prescribed, conventional niches. The allegation that "there's nothing out there to help the men" is unfounded. Our continental organization, UUMeN, possesses a growing stock of literature available to assist our local tribes in starting and sustaining men's programming. The challenge is to order, then use it.

Think about it: if women and children's programs fizzled out or were non-existent in our congregations, wouldn't there be an understandable outcry?

Shouldn't every boy who is a part of our religious education effort know that he's on a lifespan quest accentuating "positive liberal religious masculinity" and that he's surrounded and guided by exemplary men (other than simply his own father or brothers) who can serve as challengers and comforters for his religious journey? This is of no minor relevance to me personally since our seven-year-old grandson Trevor, and his younger brother Owen, attend our home church. And what about the vast importance of girls and women experiencing mature men in our Unitarian Universalist communities?

These are troublesome times for girls and boys. External influencers such as the media produce rigid and spurious gender growth options for our youngsters. Cooper Thompson tells of an exercise in sexual identity that he uses with elementary school age children. They're asked, "if you woke up tomorrow and discovered that you were the opposite sex from the one you are now, how would you and your life be different?"

He and his co-workers report the following responses as fairly typical of boys: "If I were a girl, I'd be stupid and weak as a string"; "I'd have to wear makeup, cook, be a mother, and yucky stuff like that"; "I'd have to hate snakes. Everything would be miserable"; "If I were a girl, I'd kill myself." Those are pitiful, scary answers. We must do better by the boys and girls whom we companion on the road toward their adulthood. And wouldn't it prove an empathic exercise for men to wrestle with their own engendered beings as well: "If I woke up tomorrow as a woman, how would my life be different?"

Again I say, the church exists essentially to assist its members (in this case, men) in deepening themselves in order to change the world. As religious leader James Dittes proclaims: "Men should not have to look outside the church to find support and direction for living the manhood for which they were created. This conversion from a worldly definition to a self-definition open to the abundant riches of God's creation—this is the church's business."

Our central concern can't be merely attracting more men to our ranks. That's critical, but once they arrive, we sorely need vital programming that speaks directly to the personal, social, and spiritual needs of men *qua* men. Remember, there's a handsome payoff: in benefiting individual men, we'll thicken the spiritual web of our individual Unitarian Universalist congregations, as well as strengthen our overall movement.

But an even greater dividend exists. It's our discernment, as members of UUMeN, that if enough men decide to mature internally and prophetically—that is, become brothers—then the realms in which we hold power will be changed for the better. If enough men reject the oppressive and limiting stereotypes of the traditional male role, if enough men forswear the ways in which we violate personhood of others and self, if enough men become pliable rather than unyielding, then the nature of our given global reality will radically alter.

In becoming different kinds of fathers and partners, colleagues and friends, men will be committing social justice acts of immense reverberation. In sum, our brothering mission is not only to assist men in their personal or spiritual growth or merely to produce increased gender balance in our religious tribes, but also principally to evolve the kind of mature masculinity that will produce a gentler, more just society, yea, universe.

You may have your own equivalency for "mature" masculinity. A member of our local church and professor of religious studies at the University of San Diego, Evelyn Kirkley, proffers the phrase "liberative masculine spirituality." I like it, for we Unitarian Universalists, at our truest, are both liberal in thought and liberating in action, or as Evelyn puts it: "liberative."

Call it mature or liberative masculinity, our recommendation is unmistakable: *save the males by converting them to brothers!* And to achieve that feat right where we're planted—in our Unitarian Universalist tribes.

Our religious forebrother Ralph Waldo Emerson often suggested that "God has need of a person here," whenever there was a specific duty to accomplish. Well, there's currently a dire need not merely for "a few good men," to borrow the United States Marines phrase, but for a mature brothering presence in every one of our Unitarian Universalist homes.

Males Are Primary Carriers and Targets of Violence

> Gender is the single, most obvious and intractable differ-
> ence when it comes to violence in America. Men and boys
> are responsible for 95% of all violent crimes in this coun-
> try. The belief that violence is manly is not a trait carried
> on any chromosome. It's not juiced by testosterone (half
> of all boys don't fight, most don't carry weapons, and very
> few actually kill). It's, unfortunately, taught to our boys.
>
> —Michael Kimmel

Our modern society is increasingly chaotic and violent. There's an indisputable upsurge in the amount of violence on film and in the streets, between countries and within schools. The male role in perpetrating and perpetuating the systemic violence in the world is undeniable.

Look at who conceived and executed the terrorist attacks on September 11 and look at who produced the counter-terrorist response in Afghanistan. Look at the leadership that initiated a pre-emptive strike against Iraq. Bush-men have proven to be adult bullies dead-set on throwing the first punch in the fight against the infamous tough guy, albeit smaller and less powerful, Saddam Hussein.

President Bush, early on, uttered what journalist Matthew Rothschild calls "one of the grossest obscenities imaginable: 'War may be unavoidable.'" Rothschild goes on: "War is almost always avoidable. In the case of Iraq, it is particularly avoidable, since Iraq has not attacked the United States and is in no position to do so. It's only 'unavoidable' because Bush so desperately wants to go to war." Which, of course, he did.

This very belief that violence is unavoidable creates a self-fulfilling prophecy. Because we envision violence to be inevitable, that's what we pursue; we erase from our minds the possibility of surviving through aggressive cooperation.

Bush has even personalized this war effort by declaring that Hussein tried to kill his dad, so he's seeking retribution as a just avenger.

Additionally, our current administration contends that an Iraqi war would furnish our nation with a chance to regain the masculinity we lost in Vietnam. The whole scenario depicts twisted masculinity run amok.

I urge readers to see Michael Moore's savagely funny, sad, and horrifying documentary of America's love affair with guns and violence. *Bowling For Columbine* takes off from the massacre at Columbine High School in Littleton, Colorado to investigating the links between guns, killing, and culture all over the world.

Bowling for Columbine reminds me of a recent cartoon that depicts figures from apes to men with clubs, then spears, then guns, and the final body bears an automatic rifle, with "gun culture" emblazoned across his torso, and is seen to be stepping off a cliff into the abyss. The title of the cartoon is "Devolution of Mankind."

Moore's film uncompromisingly deals with institutional racism, corporate violence, even contains a confrontive interview with Charlton Heston, unyielding advocate of the National Rifle Association. It closes by unflinchingly recounting the tragic context of the horrendous incident of a 6-year-old boy killing a 5-year-old girl at school with a handgun in Flint, Michigan. This is a painfully necessary film for families to view, then discuss, together.

Men inflict massive violence against women and children, against other men, and against ourselves. We are wounders and wounded of the highest order. I say wounded, because men suffer greatly in a world that trains us, then rewards us, as primary carriers and targets of rampaging violence.

Men and boys are hurting in ways that often go unrecognized. Andrew Kimbrell, in *The Masculine Mystique*, reports that boys are twice as likely as girls to suffer from autism and eight times more likely to be treated for hyperactivity. Two-thirds of special education is devoted to boys, and 60 percent of high school dropouts are male. An estimated 270,000 of our veterans are homeless—70 percent of the homeless being single men.

The prison situation is deplorable and degrading to men in general and men of color in particular. Nearly two million people are now behind bars in the United States. Two-thirds of those sent to prison are convicted of nonviolent crimes. And our criminal justice system is racist to the core. While African-Americans make up only 13% of drug users, they account for 35% of arrests, 55% of convictions, and 74% of those doing time for drug related sentences. And we wonder why there are more African-American men in prison than in college!

And some are so young and so hopeless, since it's been a game of survival for males of color since birth. Beneath the prison swagger lies a young man's deep fears and regrets. "Sorry, Mom, for what I've done, but remember I'm still your son," reads the tattoo on one cellmate's forearm.

On another front, men are trapped between a commitment to provide for their families and the desire to sustain emotional closeness with those they love. Nearly 80% of married men with preschool children are employed full-time. Half of all marriages disintegrate, with men receiving custody of the children in less than 20 percent of contested divorce actions. And then immature masculinity breeds absent non-custodial fathers. One out of five divorced fathers sees his children as little as once a year. Lots of men have simply lost hope about their roles as fathers.

But whether men's violence is societally sanctioned or not doesn't get us off the hook. Our male gender ultimately must do its share to break this cycle of devastation. As Unitarian Universalist colleague Ron Mazur puts it: "The ultimate male power is to say *No* to violence." This means resisting beliefs and ceasing behaviors that violate the personhood of others. To put it another way, we must evolve a religious community and larger society that is male-enhancing, that affirms masculine energy and gift but never at the expense of anyone or anything else in creation.

While men are the primary carriers of the virus, it's not an incurable disease. Men can change, but it will take a revolution, an ongoing one.

Perverted Patriarchy Is a Culprit

Perverted patriarchy is a culprit—what Unitarian feminist author Charlotte Perkins Gilman called "our androcentric culture" in her 1911 book entitled *The Man-Made World*. But two complicating observations need to be made at the outset.

First, it must be acknowledged that patriarchy has undoubtedly made huge contributions in culture-building throughout human history.

13

Second, while patriarchy literally refers to "the rule of fathers," modern Western culture has been marked by the physical absence of fathering energy and gift. Lamentably, tyrants, not fathers, have dominated the social scene.

So, the brothering imperative is to dismantle a certain kind of patriarchal system—one where irresponsible, misogynistic, and despotic male bullies rule the roost. Such hypermasculinized patriarchy has not only devastated the lives of women and children but also caused ruinous damage to the psychological development and socialization of boys. Hence, the enemy of mature masculinity is not women or other men, but a diabolical patriarchal system that has been, with few exceptions, the normative paradigm in the West from at least the second millennium B.C.E. to the present.

The goal that mature sisters and brothers pursue is authentic coexistence of all living entities.

The masculinity I espouse isn't interested in blaming or shaming my male gender but in calling it to accountability. Authentic brothering never sinks to what the media calls male-bashing and scholars reference as "misandry" or prejudice against the masculine *per se*. The brothering path stands over against the myriad of derisive masculine images flooding the collective consciousness of a modern culture where there can exist TV shows entitled "Men Behaving Badly" and popular essayists composing articles which scornfully ask: "Are Men Obsolete?"

Brothering neither glorifies nor denigrates men but posits a realistic vision and program for our tomorrows. Unitarian Universalism is a life-affirming faith, one given neither to pessimism nor to optimism but to hopefulness, and hopefulness creates change. Brothering summons men to become our best—most emotionally and morally mature—selves, on the path toward effecting an equitable social order and husbanding an ecologically balanced Creation.

Nor are we comparing wounds with women. Men often try to defend or explain ourselves by asserting that women commit their share of violence. Of course, that's the case. In fact, statistics relate that the number of girls under age 18 arrested for a violent act has jumped 80% in recent years. But our job as men isn't to decry women but to prod ourselves. We can't set women's homework assignments, but we can clarify, then fulfill, our own.

Stopping Violence against Women and Children

Every 15 seconds, a woman is beaten by her husband or partner. Batterers in the U.S. kill four women every day. In the past 10 years the incidence of rape has risen four times faster than the total crime rate. In America rape is now the most pervasive violent crime. The hidden tragedy of violent assaults against women is that the vast majority of these crimes go unreported, uninvestigated, and unpunished. By the end of the next six minutes, a woman will be sexually assaulted.

Men don't want to keep hearing such horrific statistics; neither do women. But psychic numbing wreaks internal havoc and produces apathy. These are live people: women whom we know. They are our mothers, our partners, and our sisters . . . and to my own grievous, familial despair, both of my daughters have endured sexual violence.

In her 1997 book *Anything We Love Can Be Saved: A Writer's Activism*, Alice Walker recounts a conversation with Samuel Zan, the general secretary of Amnesty International in Ghana, which is deeply involved with African women and men dedicated to the abolition of female genital mutilation. "Alice," Zan says after a long silence, "do you know what I believe? I believe that if the women of the world were comfortable, this would be a comfortable world."

Comfortable as in safe from harm and safe for free, responsible choices . . . safe to walk the streets at night and safe to be their whole selves. I believe Zan's statement to be true—agonizingly so.

And the children, oh the children, those of this land as well as those in other parts of the world. Marian Wright Edelman, who has been a lifelong advocate for the little ones, deplores "that we permit children to be the poorest Americans. And despite our nearly 300-billion-dollar military defense, we seem not to be able to protect our children from being murdered every three hours. I believe that this great nation can keep its children safe on the streets, in their homes, and in their schools. If we do not do that, what are we about?" Perhaps the question that most directly assesses the overall health of our culture is this: "How goes it with your children?"

Yet children are too frequently, including in our own progressive congregations, ignored, marginalized, if not out-and-out devalued, no matter how noble our moral pronouncements read. A Unitarian Universalist brother mentioned to me recently that the core of his life-mission, as long as he breathes, is to make sure that the children he meets at home and on the streets will be heard, listened to, then believed. He is passionately trying to atone for a former path of blatant disregard and betrayal of children. One changing man . . . changing his corner of the world.

Horizontal Violence Is Rampant

Horizontal violence is also rampant, with men hurting, killing one another, not just in war, but intensifyingly on our streets. The lamentable fact is this: when men aren't sufficiently involved in assaulting the real societal demons, we're prone to chew upon one another, with disastrous results.

Young men are among the primary perpetrators and victims. Remember that men are victims of about 70% of all robberies and make up 70% of all other victims of aggravated assaults. Aaron Kipnis adds: "Violence against men is a form of entertainment in our culture. Boxing, football, hockey, and car racing often feature men being wounded, maimed, even killed."

Littleton, Colorado and Santee, California and other similar tragedies of wanton violence document that our American boys are in grim trouble. Unitarian Universalist activist and author Michael Gurian has written two excellent books on the subject: *The Wonder of Boys* and *A Fine Young Man*. He alleges that "our boys are crying out for help through destructive acts." Gurian's research indicates that "girls and boys each have their own equally painful sufferings."

However, having studied 30 cultures around the world, Gurian notes: "Nowhere have I seen a population of young males who have less emotional bonding and moral development than our own. . . . In recent decades, we have watched our boys become the most violent and incarcerated population of adolescent boys anywhere in the industrialized world." Indeed, our young boys are trained for dominant, often toxic, masculinity, where the governing ethos becomes "pass on the sting."

You know what adult men can do to address this horrendous crisis? We can make religious education for our boys not only friendly but also downright saving. However, one stipulation: it will require the full, active companionship of adult male leaders. We men must enflesh the compassionate imperative to assume responsibility not only for our own offspring but also for at least one child outside our clan.

Evangelicals are targeting teen boys in trouble, by luring them into football stadium rallies energized with Christian rock bands, hip-hop artists, extreme sports exhibitions, testimonials, and fast-paced videos. They're challenging hormone-raging boys to "step up to the plate" and "become warriors for Christ." While our methods and message differ markedly, we religious liberals need to do our own "stepping up to the plate" to attract, hold, and deepen the commitment of young boys and men to their family, religion, and community—hooking them up with male spiritual mentors, who will buddy them through fair and foul weather.

I'm convinced that compassionate buddying will reduce the rampant bullying in American society. Bullying today is more frequent—and much more vicious—than it was but a decade ago. And its primary perpetrators and victims are our young boys. As one ten-year-old boy bemoaned: "Mom, if you think your life is hard, you ought to be on the playground at recess." We must systematically bullyproof our schools, simply agree not to tolerate it. And we must commit to heart the words of reggae singer Bob Marley: "Remember the biggest bully you ever saw was once a baby." And still needs our firm adult hugs and boundaries every day.

Soulful, prophetic liberal religious programming provides a critical contribution toward saving the boys and young men entrusted to the care of our congregations. I'll never forget the sentiment of one adult male minister who poignantly said: "I'm primarily a professional religious educator to make the world safe (no, that's not quite possible) . . . to make the world *hospitable* for the kind of young boy that I was . . . outside, different, lonely."

17

An Epidemic of Self-Violence

Men ensnarled in self-violence pose a major epidemic as well. We die from all causes combined an average of nine years earlier than women. In 1900 the incidence of stomach ulcers was primarily among women, but today men have three to four times as many ulcers as women. Our cancer rate tops that of women by 40 percent. Testicular cancer alone has grown by 50 percent between 1970 and 1993 throughout the industrialized world. Diabetes, alcoholism, and lung cancer are all favored manly maladies, judging by the lopsided statistics.

And toss in additional emotional ailments for painful measure. We males are three times more susceptible to obsessive-compulsive neurosis, and five to ten times more likely to become psychopathic personalities than women. Ten times more likely to commit murder.

This new millennium finds too many men, across the board, suffering from what Philip Culbertson labels "gender dysphoria—an emotional state characterized by anxiety, melancholy, and restlessness . . . rooted in our genderal embodiment." Men are suppressed and repressed in multiple ways, but depressed as well—our hearts simply pressed down. And still, few men are willing to face bottled-up despondency; the majority stoically "gut it out," and often flounder, even self-destruct. Suicide rates are about four times higher for men than women.

To compound our male fragility, the Y chromosome has fallen on hard times. In the 50 years since DNA was shown to be a spiral staircase of interlocking chemicals that determine what we're made of, manhood has been tumbling down it. The Y chromosome, which derails 4-week-old embryos from their default female status onto the rocky path of maleness, is starting to look like a genetic reprobate. A recent article in the *British Medical Journal* refers to the Y chromosome as "a biological injury," although it cautions against concluding that "maleness is a genetic disorder."

I recount this disheartening news in order to animate men toward healthier work, nutritional, and exercise routines. We must graduate from self-abusive to self-affirming habits. A Yale study of men in mid-life declares that those involved in social organizations—contributing beyond their work lives and sharing emotional closeness—live fuller and longer lives than men who stuff their feelings, or merely keep to themselves. We men must not continue to volunteer to die early or violently or both. The church must become a pivotal agent for altering men's health lives for the better. If machismo kills, religion saves.

Liberative religion reminds us that self-care is our greatest resource. Resistance toward medical checkups costs lives. Edward Bartlett, senior adviser to Men's Health America, a new advocacy group, laments that "today, men spend more time doing preventive upkeep on their cars than on their own bodies." A deplorable fact. As Unitarian Universalists we affirm the inherent worth and dignity of every person—including our male bodies, male spirits, male hearts. But that's a fruitless abstraction unless men engage in systematic, aggressive self-care, what I call "temple maintenance."

Stephen Boyd, a proponent for holistic growth, challenges men to assume four basic vows with regard to our physical beings: (1) "I will stop numbing my body with. . . ."; (2) "I will nurture and care for myself as a body-self . . . recognizing the ultimate authority in such care is the body and its wisdom"; (3) "I will replenish my senses . . . realizing that because of the lack of sensory input, we men find ourselves at times depressed, enervated, and compulsive about genital sexuality"; and (4) "I will attend to and care for the earth and its creatures. Reconciliation with our body-selves calls forth reconciliation with the earth and other earth creatures."

Again, I say, for our own well-being as well as that of the entire cosmos, men must become a different kind of animal, one that has rarely been seen in human history. We must evolve from carriers of death to affirmers of life. Mature, responsible masculinity is the answer to our physical-psycho-spiritual predicament, and brothering must be intentionally advocated within our congregations. If not there, then where? If not now, when?

We Remain a Band of the Cautiously Hopeful

Remember this blunt summons to brothering is not merely to serve men but moreover to save the world. My entire premise and promise are thoroughgoingly salvational. And why not? Salvation dwells at the heart of our Unitarian Universalist gospel. As Unitarians we exclaim that every unit of existence is holy and precious and to be treated as such. As Universalists we espouse an Infinite Spirit that holds in its loving embrace the totality of Creation. And our primary male task, as I see it, is simply to resemble that gospel.

Salvational work is no idle venture, no sideline spectacle. It requires full involvement, all the way home. Changing men, changing the world is holy and hopeful work, unquestionably hard work too. Men can negotiate successfully the rocky trek from boyhood to manhood, ultimately to brotherhood. But the journey is excruciatingly arduous at times, since there are women who claim it to be impossible and men who unwittingly sabotage the adventure.

We of UUMeN remain positive and expectant about the male gender. Cynicism is treason to the spirit, and shallow optimism only fosters smug contentment. Therefore, we're chastened crusaders; we're cautiously hopeful. We believe that men can—not that we always will—but we can repent, resist, reconcile, rejoice, and renew along the road toward fullness of humanity. As bell hooks urges:

> So many people have expressed this real hard-core sense that men are never going to change. And I have thought, can you imagine the despair of black people under slavery had we felt that there was nothing about that system that was going to change, that there was nothing about white people as a group or as individuals that would change? One of my favorite statements that I say a lot is the whole notion that "what we can't imagine, can't come to be."

Following in Brother Jacob's Footsteps

History is teeming with commendable stories of men changing— seizing fresh names and housing new identities. Jacob, the deceitful one prone to trickery and subversion, dared to wrestle feverishly, all night long, with God, another man, a demon, himself, an angel, or was it some combination of these interweaving forces? And Jacob emerged from this fiercesome fray intact, with two marked changes—one external and one internal.

Jacob entered the fresh dawn with an injured leg, limping the remainder of his days as well as harboring a new name, Israel, which translates as the one "who struggles with Yahweh." What a mighty paradigm for the challenge facing men who would risk changing into brothers. Renamed and wounded, brothers hobble fearlessly into our tomorrows.

And there are modern-day transformational tales of men following in Jacob's footsteps, of men daring to become brothers. We can never tell or hear too many stories of salvation, women and men alike. They furnish the nutriments for our maturation.

One of the pillars in the local men's fellowship of First Unitarian Universalist Church in San Diego had been a truck driver for some 20 years before crashing, on the job, in a life-threatening accident. Months later, after healing well enough to re-attend church, he tearfully offered the following testimony.

> Here I am, walking, healed, whole—well, mostly whole. This device [he held up an immense steel contraption for the congregation to see] was surgically implanted in my spine to hold and stabilize the vertebrae that had to regrow.
>
> Prior to my accident, I had a fierce internal conflict I was unable to resolve. I was no longer being spiritually fulfilled by my work as a trucker. Not to sound macabre, but you might say that on April 1st I got my lucky break. My new job suddenly became healing. It has been a slow, tedious process of recovering from surgery, regaining control of bodily functions and learning to walk again, with many setbacks along the way.
>
> I want you to know that my community never failed me. All of you, especially the men from the fellowship. Thank you, all!
>
> You know, my accident stimulated thoughts of salvation, of my own soul being spared from death. I felt this

21

tremendous burden of obligation, and I didn't have a spine to carry the burden. As I lay in that hospital bed, I was being crushed by the weight, just a feeling, of the obligation for merely surviving the accident and the opportunity to heal. I had to let go.

My deeper learning came through to me, in a dream state, that I didn't have an obligation to pay, that it was a gift, that life was a gift, and all I had to do was accept it. Out of that realization it was appropriate to make the transition with a name change (from Bill to Will). I couldn't pay the bill. I didn't need to pay the bill. I could live in God's will, which is life in all its abundance. I had been given the will-power to heal and overcome this trial. So life is a gift. For me, the way to pay back a gift is to receive it with thankfulness and be willing to pass it on to others.

I've faced life crises before, but I did it without community, and not very successfully. The Men's Fellowship here is the key for me. It's been my saving community.

And here's the story of a gay man who came to our church to attend a PFLAG (Parents and Friends of Lesbians and Gays) meeting. While there he learned of our Fourth Monday evening men's discussion group. One Monday, he decided to skip PFLAG and try the brotherhood instead. He was transformed, saved, as he put it:

Two things happened. One, I saw Mr. Wonderful and knew this must be close to home! But more importantly, in discussion of the Promise Keepers one man said something about the good things they promote in spite of their policies toward gay men. I challenged that, saying that since they advocated the death of all gay men, there was nothing particularly redeeming about Promise Keepers.

At that point another man, I'd never seen before, slowly arose and pointed right at me and said with unmistakable passion, "Trust me! If there is a mortal threat on

your life, I will place my body . . . my very life between you
and that threat!"

Imagine hearing, for the first time in a life where the
world was a constant threat, another man offering his life
to defend yours!

The UU Men's Fellowship has been a sacred commu
nity for me now for 10 years. Within the Men's Fellowship
I've been saved literally, from a world of fear and dread.
I've learned how to be a brother, both receiving and giving. I've found the solid footing of genuine belonging, a
weaving together of all the strings and threads and yarns
into one fabric.

You see, every man walking the earth, harbors a tale worthy of the
telling and hearing. "If one woman ever told the whole honest truth
about her life," writes Muriel Rukeyser, "the world would split open." The
fact is that earth-shattering results also occur when men dare to reveal
their interior anguish and yearnings. I've seen it with my own eyes, heard
it with my own ears, felt it with my own arms.

"Tell Them about the Dream, Martin!"

As Gandhi urged, "We must become the changes we wish to see."
And what do our Unitarian Universalist brothering ventures see? We
behold a men's presence and path existing on every one of our church
campuses in this fresh century. Our mission is to realize that vision, yea,
to become the very change we wish to see! Again, this is not merely about
saving individual men but transforming the entire universe—starting in
our homes of worship and mushrooming from there.

We would follow in sister Susan B. Anthony's footsteps when she
wrote: "Failure is impossible." We would be so brazen as to foresee that
success is possible—perhaps not in our lifetimes, but surely in this millennium. That's our prayerful hope. That's the prize upon which our eyes
are unswervingly set.

For brothering is our highest calling as men.

I offer a closing story about Martin Luther King, Jr. It occurred 40 years ago, back in 1963, when he delivered his now-famous "I Have A Dream" speech at the March on Washington. John Lewis, one of his lieutenants, remembers the speech as being a good one but not nearly vintage King. As he moved toward the homestretch of his address, it seemed that King himself could sense that he was falling short as well. He simply hadn't locked into the power he customarily found.

Lewis was sitting near enough to hear Mahalia Jackson, who was seated just behind King, lean in as he was finishing and urged him out loud, "Tell them about the dream, Martin, tell them about the dream. . . ." And the rest, which focused upon King's dreams for the upcoming generations of black children, surely constitutes minutes of some of the finest speechmaking in American history.

Well, those of us in UUMeN have a dream too, and while it differs somewhat situationally from King's, it too would fervently lift up majestic possibilities for the little ones coming along after us, the boys and girls to whom we are bequeathing this wondrous yet wacky world.

We have a dream that men are not incurably macho, let alone violent; that we can take better care of ourselves; that we can be attentive partners, intimate friends, dauntless advocates and allies, devoted fathers and sons, peacemakers and husbandmen of the highest order.

We have a dream that both newcomers to our faith and the world at large, when they learn of Unitarian Universalism, will know that ours is a religion that dares to nourish the deeper hungers of men. Insiders and outsiders alike will recognize that our religion assists men in being both poetic and prophetic, strong and vulnerable, playful and productive. Furthermore, every male by birth can choose to become a brother and will be supported on that quest as long as he dwells in our fellowship of "freethinking mystics with hands."

We have a dream that, in due time, when today's brothers enter the ground, there will be other men taking up the torch of mature liberal religious masculinity in our local congregations and throughout the continent. In short, there will always be an active men's group present for our grandsons and their grandsons.

We hold that dream dear, we currently underwrite that vision with our own bodies and souls, and we call upon all card-carrying Unitarian Universalists to play their part in making this dream an approximate reality.

I exhort our *men* to enlist in the brothering revolution, to join the caravan of brothers, for your own salvation and for that of the entire Creation. I welcome our *women* to support healthy masculinity, to call us to accountability, to become our sisters. And I invite our *children* and *youth* to contribute their singular gifts in making this globe more just and joyful.

For, in saving the males, we do, oh yes, we do, take giant strides toward saving this single, precious cosmos.

Chapter 2: Start a Huge, Foolish Project

Start a huge, foolish project,
Like Noah.
It makes absolutely no difference
What people think of you.

—Rumi

Where Art Thou, Brother?

There's nary a local Unitarian Universalist congregation across the land that doesn't house religious education for children. And most of our tribes have programming for women and youth. Unfortunately, statistics show that only 10% of our faith communities have male-specific opportunities for spiritual nurture. Before this decade is out, is it too much to hope that we'll have 25% of Unitarian Universalist churches with programs dedicated specifically to the growth of our men?

It strikes me that every one of our parishes could profit by taking an audit to see how well we're doing in response to the heart-needs of our men. Remember the sexism, racism, and heterosexism assessments many of our congregations have undergone over the years? But don't just take my word for it; listen to some testimonies from colleagues in the field.

Our Weston, Florida minister Kenneth Beldon writes in a provocative essay entitled "O Brother, Where Art Thou?": "Women, it seems, are stepping *up* to the call to service in our congregations, while men, it appears, are stepping *out*. To say it plainly: we don't need fewer women; we do need more men."

Jaco Ten Hove, UUMeN President and parish minister in Paint Branch, Maryland, offers similar sentiments:

> Whenever I inquire about the percentage of women members at a given UU congregation, I'm usually told around 65–70%, often rising. Thus, it seems hard to dispute that men, as a whole, feel less inclined to participate in our churches, relative to the increase in women leaders and members. . . .
>
> But I prefer to approach this issue from a positive angle: How male spirituality might be drawn out. We are, after all, a religious community, and we should aim for our niche, which, in this case, would be offering something of value to men that could deepen and strengthen their religious identities. My current premise is that "every man has an inner life,". . . and I predict that as the male leaders in a UU congregation help make it safe and easy for other men to share pieces of their inner lives, that community will thrive with a gender equity to be admired.

Women leaders are seconding the motion. Melitta Haslund, a former parish minister in Santa Paula, California, addressed the men of her congregation through the newsletter:

> It has come to my awareness that there may be a need for our men to meet together for reasons other than fixing a drainpipe or sanding a banister. Each of us needs a time to talk about those difficult, joyous times with folks who have similar experiences. I have happily helped to facilitate the women's spirituality group and would be glad to offer any assistance to men who are interested in forming a group; however, facilitating it would be a different story. Brothers, attending the district-wide UU Men's Retreat might be a good starting point.

Carol Rosine, our minister in Franklin, Massachusetts, has worked long and hard over 15-plus years initiating, then supporting, men's programming in the congregation she serves. She has assisted in the formation of both discussion and support groups, as well as a men's social venture called the "Franks."

The optimal answer to attracting and holding men in our UU congregations is to provide programming that intentionally nourishes their personal and social growth, internal yearnings and external duties. But two cautions: first, men will not change appreciably by merely attending periodic retreats; and, second, altering the classic roles of male as primary provider, protector, and teacher—as *paterfamilias*—won't happen without ample, often agonizing, adjustments on behalf of everyone concerned: men, women, and children.

It's the Church's Job to Feed the Souls of Men

We're lucky, because we belong to a hopeful, renewable faith. Unitarian Universalism contends that men can alter, substantially and enduringly, through regular participation in supportive brothering clans. A healthy parish is the best place in town to push men toward self-critique without subjecting them to self-denigration. The church is a special kind of community: historically continuous, intergenerational, and a field-site for moral stretches and life transitions. In short, nothing less than a communally-based masculinity will adequately grow men's souls.

Lodges for men, from Elks to Moose, are historically grounded in social camaraderie and philanthropic outreach, worthy ventures in their own fashion, but none of them is specifically geared to tackle the spiritual needs of men. That's the job of the church, the temple, the mosque, the sangha.

Consequently, our liberal religious congregations must become trustworthy sites for men forging intimate bonds of renewal with other men. Such growth happens through discussion, support, worship, service, and retreats. When a man comes onto our church campus, he must find an open door, with something meaningful for him on the other side of the door—namely, religious growth and learning alternatives tailored for his masculine evolution. Full-service faith communities provide men with robust opportunities to become brothers.

The novelist Emile Zola wrote: "If you asked me what I came into the world to do—I will tell you. I came to live out loud!" Too few men live out loud, that is, divulge our heart secrets in open, caring circles. Shouldn't that be one of the central purposes of a religious tribe: to coax, challenge, celebrate our courage to live congruently in every region of our lives?

Brothering is not a puny, part-time endeavor. It entails men's *programming*, but more. It means having a men's *presence* on location every Sunday. At least a staffed table with literature. It signifies the construction of a *path* that may be followed by individual men in their own pace and manner, but a path nonetheless.

We may be men by birth, but we become brothers through deliberate cultivation of our masculine beings. Becoming a brother constitutes men's healthiest and holiest vocation—a calling that produces universal hopefulness for all living entities.

The brothering path constitutes both revolutionary and sacred work; in all honesty, it represents a huge, foolish project, not unlike the big, brazen one ventured by brother Noah way back when. And whether we fail or flourish over the long haul in building a viable ark, it matters not, for we men are called to faithfulness, not success.

Moreover, as Rumi implies, it doesn't really matter what people think of us, for if men truly risk this huge, foolish project I'm proposing—namely, a brothering revolution—we will be advancing on a route of justice-building and joy-sharing. Men will be living our destiny, a transpersonal mission that grants our lives incalculable purpose.

The WHAMMM Factor

Mine is not an exceptional odyssey, but, like that of every brother walking the earth, worthy of some retelling. But three admissions, at the outset, are necessary to cleanse my heart, if not clear the air. First, my story is not of one living at any margins of social acceptance but rather essentially as a card-carrying member of WHAMMM (white, heterosexual, Anglo-Saxon, middle-class, middle-age males). I didn't earn this condition (some would say predicament) of multiple entitlements; I was ushered into it by fate.

A second admission. I'm also aware that when I look into the mirror I basically see a human being, your generic person, so to speak. My class, race, and gender are hardly visible; whereas men of color tell us that they see color before maleness, before anything else. They see color and feel its attendant societally-induced stresses and disadvantages. My point is that WHAMMM constituents possess the unearned luxury of emotional space and economic freedom to work straightway on maturing our masculinity. We move relatively unencumbered in the world.

That's one reason why the men's movement, in all its variations (there are exceptions like the Million Man March) has been predominantly WHAMMMers doing their own growth, as important as that is. And, unquestionably, a sizable hunk of that growth needs to include getting to know non-WHAMMM men up-close and personal, hearing who they are and bridging with their authentic identities in ways that are respectful, not patronizing.

Here's the difference. Men of color need to know pretty much everything about the dominant "white" culture in order to navigate it (as Celie puts it in *The Color Purple*. "Can't get that white man off my eyeballs!"), while WHAMMMers can conveniently remain in relative ignorance about the variant cultures of persons of color.

But the changing world changes men, whether we're ready or not, at least in part. The 21st-century demographics of our local Unitarian Universalist tribes, especially in metropolitan areas, are starting to resemble, more and more, the diverse colors and classes and capacities in the larger world. The hegemonic masculinity of European culture, while still in ascendancy in our liberal religious fold, is loosening.

Furthermore, we can, and should, be intentional about diversifying. For example, our brothering revolution would endorse men's movement leader Michael Meade's refusal to hold any conferences unless all kinds of men, especially the marginalized, are specifically welcome and present.

Another reflection. Not only are these categories unjust to the oppressed, but by allowing some people to flourish precisely through dominating others, all human beings are diminished. Yes, WHAMMMers suffer too in the oppression we sustain. Our ignorance, our arrogance, and our moral bankruptcy hurt us.

As Mary Elizabeth Hobgood, in her book *Dismantling Privilege: An Ethics of Accountability*, cogently observes: "The solution is a politics of solidarity grounded in the realization that no one is free until all are free—and that only by being accountable for privilege and working together to establish equity for all can we truly be a just society." And I would add: a joyful one as well.

A final admission. My particular WHAMMM journey has been quite sheltered. To be sure, I've not hidden out in a cocoon. I've known illness, divorce, misconduct, death, insecurity, and inadequacy, but most of my torments have been internally generated, not externally imposed. One quick example. In 1965 I went to Selma, at the urging of Dr. King, to assist disenfranchised African-Americans in the push for civil rights legislation. Yet I didn't live, as did they, with daily threats to my dignity. I was slandered and spit upon for a week, not a lifetime. I was a visitor. I left Selma.

Mine has been a privileged place, even if punctuated by occasional detours and disturbances. But it's also true that members of WHAMMM are not totally immune to the slings and arrows of misfortune. Examples abound. Plenty of WHAMMMers are trapped in depression. Or they've beaten others and been beaten themselves. Or they've incurred the indelible scars of both military trauma and triumph. Or they've lost their jobs in the ongoing quest for affirmative action, a program they sometimes both understand and applaud. And their stories are stories to be heard, their bodies are bodies to be embraced, whenever they choose to join our fellowship and pour forth their oft-buried interiors.

At the close of all our brotherhood conclaves, I invite men to join hands, as is comfortable. But I consciously leave an opening between the next guy and me. The circle is intentionally broken, as a reminder that there are men who aren't in our company: men too frightened to appear, men who don't feel welcome, men who don't possess the time, resources, or wheels to attend, and so on. My closing words, before our benedictory chant, are: "May our circle always remain open for yet another man on the road toward becoming a brother."

Maturing from Boyhood to Brotherhood

All any of us can do is speak from our souls, rooted in our own soil. Hence, some portions from my male chronicle.

I was a shy little guy, barely opening my mouth until I went to kindergarten. I didn't feel unduly frightened or dwarfed, at least not consciously; perhaps I was merely pondering things in my heart, like the biblical Mary. Yet finding my voice, both literally and vocationally, has been one of my hard-won blessings as a male.

Despite increasing verbal facility in the primary grades, I continued to shake and shiver, if not freeze up, when speaking before authority figures or simply outside the home. I remember entering speech contests as a teenager, mainly as a counterbalance to bone-deep, sweaty fright in voicing my views. I pushed myself and was shoved by others as well in order to confront my demons of outside judgment and potential rejection.

I was a good boy, liked by both adults and peers, and I didn't want to disturb my rather snug (probably smug too) state by doing or saying something objectionable. So, whenever I did speak out loud, especially in the presence of adults, it was to please them. I was your classic placater, and still am—in both the best and worst senses: a gentle-man, a nice guy who adroitly sidesteps conflict and difficulty. Sweet but susceptible to being syrupy.

After my opening Minns Lecture during the fall of 2002, when I dealt with some heavy material around men's violence, I not only felt sweaty and unduly anxious during the talk, but I also had trouble sleeping that night. I kept mulching what I didn't say or what I said poorly. You see, I'm still wrestling with being a good guy who dares to say tough things!

When Robert Bly says in *Iron John*, "Is there anything dangerous to do around here?" the best equivalent I can usually muster reads: "Is there anything adventurous to do around here?" And my adventures are invariably well-calculated and guarded.

Although I've developed into an active, occasionally forceful, profeminist, gay-affirming, male-positive, racially inclusive voice for men, it's real hard for me to stand near the direct line of fire, or be labeled a bad guy. And it's relatively easy for me to speak out against our own crimes as men; since that way I'm occupying the moral high ground, plus usually reaping the praise of progressive women.

Strident, cutting statements like that of the radical gay feminist John Stoltenberg, "If you ain't catchin' shit, you ain't doin' shit!" still unnerve and haunt me to the core. Oh, the eternal and infernal trek from being a good boy to a mature man.

A further aside. Some of the publicity for my second Minns Lecture, I learned too late, misprinted a key word. It invited, men and women alike, to come learn how to start and sustain a *bothering* (not brothering) path in your local congregation. I laugh, in retrospect, at this goof, but it was clearly a prescient blunder, for men who truly become brothers in any revolutionary sense, become bothers as well—nagging bothers to society as well as to their own life-flow. But, as I'm confessing up front, becoming a brother who bothers, disturbs, and stirs up shit is hardly my preferred way of moving in the world.

Back to my tale. As a student, I was outer-directed, working more to charm others than to match my own standards. As an athlete, I was skilled in sports but lacked the hard-nosed drive necessary to excel. In my teen years into early adulthood, I remember frequently saying "I'm sorry, I'm sorry," after I fouled someone in basketball, almost as a mindless mantra, clearly apologizing in inappropriate fashion.

As a mate, I'm still conflict-avoidant, rarely fighting at all, let alone fairly and firmly. As a parent and grandparent, I confess to being a faint-hearted disciplinarian.

And as a singer, my muffled voice has only been freed since my father's confident, expansive voice was silenced when he died in 1987. For whatever reasons, it matters not, my voice reaches belly-ward now. At least sometimes, when it's not hoarse or congested.

And so it goes.

My growing edges are mine and yours are yours. Comparisons are odious; the last thing we need to do as men is try to out-confess or out-steeple one another. As a man you will need to set your own growth agenda, but central to my becoming a more balanced masculine presence in the world has been migrating, ever so slowly, from convenient silence to

34

courageous forthrightness, from being an habitual stroker to an infrequent shameless agitator. My gnawing bone has been to retain my temperamental softness without turning spineless—to give up chickenheartedness, once and for all. Yes, every knight has his own dragons to elude, slay, or make peace with.

A Painful Personal Passage

When I went through a divorce in 1972, at the age of 30, it was improbable that I should seek the solace and support of men, but I did. Like most men, I had been notoriously dependent upon women for my social, sensual, and sexual energy. Like most men (even gay men), I had few male friends and those were relatively shallow. Like most men, I was pretty insecure around and scared of other males, especially those strong, hefty guys in charge.

Too many men still avoid seeking help (especially from other men), even when we're despairingly trapped by a lost job, a shattered love, a physical injury, and a persistent shame. Typically, men choose to lick our wounds in solitude. So I'm not sure why I reached out to males during this time of grave emotional need, but I did, and it proved a wise move indeed. For, ever since savoring the deep caresses of male friendship, some thirty years ago now, I've never turned my back on men. And I never will. Indeed, now I regularly turn toward men for gentle embraces, even swift kicks.

Once connected, I've become an unapologetic believer in the benefits of brothering. Make that, an unabashed crusader for men's intimacy and ultimacy. In fact, I started my first men's support group during this season of personal turmoil and trauma.

I recently re-read the talks I gave to community groups in 1973 concerning gender identity and growth, and although our embryonic men's movement was basically reactive to the more vigorous and developed women's movement, I still concur with much of what I penned. I acutely needed, at that juncture in my life, to share serious, candid, trustworthy male conversation and companionship beyond sex and sports, business and beer.

I still do. And I'm hardly alone in that need.

M.A.L.E.—The Ark Gets Underway

In 1973 we West Coast men were guinea pigs or pioneers, take your pick, there being little psycho-spiritual fare available for men who were on the grow. This was pre-Warren Farrell and Herb Goldberg, let alone Robert Bly and Ellis Cose. And religion was doing little to feed our souls. So a few of us set out to build an ark, to undertake a huge, foolish project in the direct lineage of Noah. We named our structure M.A.L.E. (Men's Awareness Liberation Effort).

M.A.L.E. spelled a pompous acronym to be sure, although I recall an early men's group with the same designation back East (the Mid-Atlantic Literary Edification Society) that sounded more obtuse and equally pretentious. But Unitarian Universalist men were at least risking our own growth apart from (not over against) women and children. We were clarifying our own identities as men *qua* men, not simply as partners, providers, and fathers. It wasn't easy—pacesetting work never is—and while we were clumsy to be sure, often chided and parodied, the path we were hewing was the right one, no question about it.

Back then, both genders stumbled a lot in each other's liberational presence. Actually still do. Here's but a modest example of ineptitude from three decades ago.

I was invited to speak on an intergender panel before a Southern California crowd of family counselors on the theme: "A Man's Response to Women's Lib." The coordinator of the program, in her letter to me, inadvertently penned: "We're delighted that you've consented to participate in our program. The evening promises to be an exciting one, and you may want to invite friends and relatives to watch you perform." Whoops! I winced then and still do at the choice of the loaded term: "Perform!" I mean, intergender dialogue was new, scary territory for men to enter in 1973. So, while I was willing to swap notes on a panel, indeed share my embryonic views, "perform" wasn't descriptive of what I was either ready or willing to do. Men have been perennially pegged to be performers—with our minds and bodies, verbally and sexually.

As women were climbing down from pedestals, we men were trying to climb off stages. This program, an inaugural event of sorts, was not the time to produce, protect, or perform some more. Just sharing would be challenge enough, thank you.

But women and men can't be too critical of one another; pioneers will regularly say and do awkward, even hurtful, things on the road toward increasing justice and joy. Sometimes deliberate but usually unintentional. What really matters, in retrospect, is that what we introduced with M.A.L.E. was neither faddish nor fatuous, however occasionally foolish. And that evening, while a bit rocky, went pretty well.

In fact, some of what I said that night contains wisdom I'm still trying to emulate:

> If we men want to know what our blind spots or sore spots are with respect to women's oppression, then I invite us to ask ourselves: When do I as a man feel anger, threat, embarrassment concerning who women are and what they do to, for, and with me?
>
> Given this statement, let me move on to say that more of us men are blind to our own suppression as adult males. Our primary gift to women, ourselves, other men, and children is to free ourselves from the masculinity trap (both subtle and blatant) to which we allow ourselves to be enslaved.
>
> Additionally, I would say tonight that maleness doesn't derive from femaleness, so men must form our own identities per se, risk our own voices. We would seek to be fuller, freer, more flexible adult male humans and begin by facing our own pain and assuming our own pride and power.
>
> With sensitive support from men, women can be aided on their journey to liberation. With sensitive support from women, men can be aided on their journey to liberation.
>
> The crux of the struggle, however, is that I as a male am primarily in charge of my own liberation and women

their own. If we can get clear about who is ultimately responsible for whom and who can be supportive of and involved with whom, then we should really have something freeing for all humans. And imagine the great stuff our children will get in on!

M.A.L.E. advocates were essentially concerned about changing male reality both *internally*—shedding suppressive male stereotypes—and *externally*—stopping our oppressive male behavior toward women, children, and other men. We wanted to become more emotionally expressive and ethically worthy men. Plus we were simply hurting, and many, like myself, undergoing life-altering distress. However, substantive change doesn't come smoothly, for, as they say, only wet babies willingly change their situation. The rest of us usually hanker to have our recurrent discomfort go away without having to make any actual changes.

Yet I've held tenaciously ever since, even if haltingly, to self-change, because I've believed, from my head to my toes, that when men, culture's ascendant power-brokers, dare to make additions and corrections to our living minutes, the entire globe will undergo seismic shifts. Changing men changes the world.

Such was the driving vision of this little band of Unitarian Universalist brothers back in 1973. This basic impulse and imperative remain valid in 2003.

A Shameless Agitator for Men

Ever since those initial forays I've aspired to be a dogged ambassador for men's soulful and prophetic growth. I awoke to the realization that, as a man, I should focus primary energy upon the privilege, plight, and promise of my own genderal embodiment: becoming the healthiest version of masculinity possible! Naturally, I'm related to others, but I'm responsible for myself.

My missionary zeal on behalf of authentic brothering has converted some men to the cause, awakened others, and repelled a few. But I've kept on course, believing that if there exists a critical mass of mature men in our movement and beyond, we will contribute toward the creation of a more just and enjoyable globe. Plus I've never abandoned the conviction that, for better and for worse, we must engage the brothering revolution with the chosen clans with whom we have cast our fortunes. You always bring it home.

Consequently, moving from Pasadena, California to Davenport, Iowa, I continued my brotherhood work there, with a jolt from a man in my church. It's been my experience that our changing is activated more often by external crisis or prod than by our own internal desire or good will. Remember Francis David's pivotal cry in the 16th century: "Semper reformanda" literally meant "always in need of being reformed." In other words, Unitarian Universalists are prone to cowardice and must bank on outside agents pressing us, whether screaming or receptive, into changes frequently beyond either our expectation or our grasp.

Such a moment occurred for me in Davenport, when Edward rushed up after the worship service and challenged me right there on the chancel: "Damn it, Tom, your sermons have dealt with most every imaginable social oppression except the one I suffer daily. I dare you to dig deep into your conscience and goad you to preach about homosexuality and homophobia—then launch a gay-straight dialogue in the Quad Cities, starting right here in our church. I'll match your bravery with my own. Hey, let's come out of our respective closets and do something truly religious, even revolutionary, for folks here in the Iowa cornfields!" Edward's challenge reminds me of what an African-American brother said to me years later: "If you're willing to deal with racism, your own as well as that in our Unitarian Universalist movement, then I'll gladly meet you halfway!"

Well, Edward was persuasive and I was converted, for all time. As the Zen Buddhists say: "When you're ready, your *roshi* will appear." Edward was the first of many teachers, in various guises, who have since graced my life on the matter of crashing barriers and constructing bridges between gay and straight men, then with bisexual men, now transgender folks.

Edward and I started a scathingly honest dialogue process that I've continued for decades, confronting fears and fostering trust across sexual orientation lines. It's been a process full of mutual awkwardness, anger, and acceptance. Yet once Edward launched me, I've seldom strayed from the path.

But it was upon return to California, when Carolyn and I were called to be team ministers in San Diego in 1978, that opportunities opened up to revolutionize the milieu for men in our local parish life. Carolyn has supported my efforts from the beginning, even as she has done her own work with women. She's been my unyielding soul-mate in the quest for gender justice and joy, goading and cheering me on as needful.

Additionally, my father died in 1987, and then shortly thereafter my beloved father-in-law also entered the ground. "They left me the earth," as the Navajos say, and my ministry to men plunged deeper and soared wider.

In fact, the very night my dad stopped breathing, I'll always treasure the gift I received from another man in our congregation. A true brother. It was Christmas Eve around 6:00 p.m. when I received news of my father's death. I immediately asked Carolyn to take total charge of our ample ministerial duties that night while I drove, weeping the whole way, from San Diego to Los Angeles (a 2½-hour drive) to comfort and be comforted by my mom.

Back at our church, during the midnight Christmas eve service, Raymond, a member who but a few years earlier had been wrongfully charged with killing his wife, and whom I had faithfully visited in jail until his release, strode slowly to our liturgical trencher, lit a candle, and said: "This one's for Pastor Tom. He was there for me when I was imprisoned; it's my turn to stand for him during his grief!" And such is the nature of brothering.

Brothering isn't the only song I sing, but it's become a foundational melody. At the highest common denominator, I'm a man and compelled to tell the plain story of my incontrovertible yearning to become a bona fide brother.

Another Kind of Intimacy

> Home, home on the range,
> where the feel and the touch are so strange,

where seldom is heard
an emotional word,
and the MEN are so lonely all day.

—Joe Fisher

We need same sex friends because there are types of validation and acceptance that we receive only from our gender mates. There is much about our experience as men
that must be shared with, and understood by, other men.
There are stories we can tell only to those who have wres-
tled in the dark with the same demons and been wounded by the same angels. Only men understand the secret
fears that go with the territory of masculinity.

—Sam Keen

Whereas our physical incarnation may be maleness, our spiritual
vocation is brotherhood. Brothering is an intentional choice, revisioned
daily, to relate to men, women, and children, indeed all reality, with the
eyes of compassion and the hands of justice. This conscious, radical
choice constitutes our ultimate challenge as men. Søren Kierkegaard went
to the heart of the mature masculine quest when he translated Socrates'
admonition "know thyself" as "choose thyself." In short, the core of the
brothering journey is to determine precisely the kind of men we want to
become . . . moment by moment, decision by decision.

There are two conventional ways we've acted as males throughout
history: either as lords and masters in charge or as underlings executing
the command of superiors. Both extremes have produced considerable ill
effects for society and men as well. We need to exemplify liberative attitudes and behaviors of manhood—what I call the way of brothering:
where men treat self and others with fundamental respectfulness.

Journalist Roger Rosenblatt writes that "men are programmed to be
isolated from one another and that aloneness is our natural state. Silence
in male friendship is our way of being alone with each other." Hogwash!

41

Quietude isn't our only mode of connecting with our own gender. Men are not constitutionally incapable of intimate bonding with other men through soulful word and caring touch.

Certainly, men are socialized to lead fiercely independent lives, yet as a member of our UU Men's Fellowship in San Diego once confessed, "I'm a self-made man, but if I had to do it over again, I'd call in others." All is not lost for this particular individual, for Peter is now fortified by the quickening embrace of responsive brothers in one of our dozen men's support circles.

The word integrity means "whole and undivided," and Unitarian Universalist brothers would rebuke the maverick mentality and instead seek to become whole, not divided or split from our peers. Wholeness banks unalterably upon men forging healthy mature bonds . . . becoming brothers.

Transformative masculinity necessitates men migrating from solitariness to solidarity across the gulfs of age, profession, gender, theology, race, orientation, ability, and class that continue to segregate men from men. Brothering occurs when men gather together to care for and confront each other. As Michael Meade rightly remarks:

> Without some sense of genuine group, too easily the individual man falls asleep or gives up. The history of men, of animals, and of learning has to do with groups, with common effort. A man can risk more exploration of his potential and of his grandiosity—he can risk more encounters with grandeur—when connected to other men who can reduce him when necessary and encourage him when needed.

Men have classically related to one another *side by side* at work and *back-to-back* in the military. Undoubtedly, in the life of a church, there will be times for men to relate through undertaking a common project or competing together on a softball team. These remain honorable ways for men to socialize. Furthermore, they often furnish the entree for many men to feel sufficiently comfortable with one another to disclose pieces of their personal stories.

But there exists a third, albeit under-practiced, mode of male intimacy: relating *face-to-face*. Much healing remains to be achieved between men, because we've been pounding upon or climbing over or even destroying one another ever since Cain snuffed out his brother Abel. Men need to learn more respectful ways to be brothers—not our brother's boss, lackey, or keeper, but our brother's brother. There are male-based fears and hopes that are more properly shared staring directly into the countenance of one's brother. We owe a "terrible loyalty" to our own gender, and payment is long overdue.

Three cardinal rules follow when men pursue face-to-face intimacy with one another: speak honestly, be brief, and listen from the heart. In due course, those three basic guidelines will enable men to brother at astonishingly deep levels.

Countless Explanations, No Excuses

However, men consistently eschew brothering circles by decrying the lack of time. This furnishes an explanation but no excuse, for I know few modern men (or women), even retirees, with oodles of spare time. Our brothering rejoinder to resistant men is simple: "The rest of your life will be unspeakably enriched by the moments you spend up-close and caring with men. Go ahead, check it out, talk to men who participate in same-sex kinship circles. They'll testify that everyone else (including the women and children in their lives) benefits from their in-depth disclosure with other men." An evening of intimacy with other men will recharge a good week's worth of enriched life at home and work. The dividends are real.

We basically challenge reluctant men to give us credence—which, of course, is no small feat, for men trusting men lies at the crux of the revolution.

Other men lament that our male species is futilely competitive, even combative. Of course, supremacy struggles can devastate brotherly ties and only confirm what ideologically militant feminists may fantasize: "Let them clobber themselves into submission." It's no secret, inter-male history is marred by self- and other-destruction, but masculinity per se is not a hopeless disease. We've learned immaturity; we can outgrow it. We can work, play, and share intimately and productively with our own gender. Give peace a chance, give brothering a chance!

In truth, brothering can unveil a rare and precious jewel that radiates joy throughout the rest of our life-connections. As colleague James Ishmael Ford notes: "Most Zen koans end with 'and she was enlightened' but some close with 'and he became more intimate.'" Yes, men are inherently capable of creating and sustaining deep, intimate bonds of brotherhood. "Taste and see," as the Hebrew scriptures urge.

But healing our male-male wounds won't occur through noble intentions or prayerful attitudes. It doesn't occur through osmosis. It happens only by spending ample time sharing our aches and aspirations, our transparent stories, as peers in non-competitive, nurturing places. It takes real effort and demands a "deep seat," as the Buddhists say.

Men also confess to being frightened of other men. Many of us are, and often with good reason. But embraced in safe, unhurtful circles, men can entertain the transformative gift of trust from other men—the building block of authentic brothering. Safe doesn't mean cuddly, or only soothing, although God knows men need to hold and be held. Safe signifies men doing emotional work, not with a hard hat so much as a firm heart. Safe denotes being sufficiently secure so that a man can face his caged and uncaged demons, as well as descend into long-buried ashes, arising often strangely cleansed and more whole.

Another excuse arrives. Men also protest that our gender can best, if not only, relate in a personal fashion with women. Again, that's a stereotypic straitjacket that multitudes of men have shattered with male-specific sharing. The proof is in the pudding.

Actually, mixed company often derails men and women from experiencing the necessary camaraderie for developing our distinctive souls. I challenge all men to answer these questions: Why benefit from the resources and gifts of only half the human race? Why spend all our waking time only with adults and bypass the children? The whole world needs the fullness of each of us engaging everyone in sight.

Consequently, women and men (transgender folks will choose their own optimal growth-circles) must labor independently but alongside one another to create a globe of greater gender justice and joy. As author-activist Alice Walker comments: "As a womanist, I am committed to survival and wholeness of entire people, male and female. I am not a separatist, except periodically for health."

More Salvation Stories

Both of the following stories were voiced during worship services, the prime time of the Beloved Community. If such public occasions carry saving power, you can imagine the depth of healing that also occurs in the more private milieu of covenantal men's circles in our congregations.

Here's a portion of what George courageously shared in our midst:

> In early childhood I suffered some wounds that are common among male children in our culture. This included an absent father and a brother who was at best a negative role model. In addition, I discovered that the way I felt toward other boys was anathema, and must be hidden forever, even from my own self. I was sent to a boarding school at age 14, and there I looked for a father or a brother. Finding neither, I realized I was alone and on my own.
>
> My life became a balancing act of copying those around me in hopes of being accepted and approved, maybe even loved. But I was forever careful not to let anyone know who I was inside. I put together an apparently good life, but there was always something missing, a vast void between me and other people, especially between me and other men.
>
> When I was still a stranger here at First Church, a man on the patio table asked me what I was looking for. I said some kind of structure within which I could learn to grow spiritually. He replied: "That's exactly what we do here in the Men's Fellowship." I've been a part of the UUMF ever since. I've found myself surrounded with brothers.
>
> On several occasions, when one or another of these brothers came too close, I tried to chase them away. I

learned instead how to stay at the table and to apologize and be forgiven. Living alone has lost its loneliness, because there's always a brother who will help. There have been cards and calls and hot food and home visits and hospital visits and dog walks. Whether it's pneumonia, the death of a beloved friend from AIDS, or a broken toe, a brother has been there. Another brother has made a habit of phoning me regularly to inquire about my physical and about my mental and spiritual health.

Can you imagine what it means to be brothered for the first time? The immense power and comfort of that?

And from my brothers in the Fellowship, I've learned to use the word "I" to speak my truth, to speak for myself not for others, and to speak from my heart. I've learned from my brothers here at church that, until I share my secrets, I'm not safe from them, but among my brothers, it's truly safe to share whatever I need to share.

The work of our UU Men's Fellowship is the process of renewal, and the result for me has been incredible healing and wholeness. Amen and Blessed be.

A second testimony comes from a young adult in our Men's Fellowship in San Diego. He shared his heart-soaked odyssey on Sunday morning as well.

Real men don't get nervous. Real men don't get scared. Real men never cry. Well, I'm nervous and scared, and in the next few minutes I will likely cry. My name is Mark Alan Penney. I'm 30 years old. I'm the son of retired Marine Corps Captain John Penney. I'm especially nervous because my father, my brothers, and my girlfriend are here today.

I've played baseball in front of Dad for years. Ever since my first cap league game some 23 years ago, I remember my Dad at those games. Later when I would pitch at Oceanside High, he would come straight from work to see my games. He would stand behind the back-stop, watching me as I warmed up. He would cross his arms and lean against the fence, and he wouldn't leave before the game was over. It felt unbelievably good having him there.

Yes, I'm nervous and scared, because the chain link fence that separated us while I played baseball is not here this morning.

When I joined the UU Men's Fellowship I had no idea what would be waiting for me near the end of the year. In September, my mother was suddenly diagnosed with cancer, and one month later, died on October 13th at the San Diego Hospice.

I owe to these men, the men of my support group and the men of the UUMF, a huge debt. During this difficult time they supported me while my mom was dying. I know it embarrasses Jack Schmidt when I tell this story, but he and I staffed together at the men's retreat right after my mom passed away. When everyone left and we were doing cleanup, Jack stopped me from what I was doing and gave me a hug.

He asked, "how do you keep it all together after having just lost your mom?" I answered with something like, "I can handle it, it's no big deal." I wanted to get back to my busy-work, and started to pull away, but Jack wouldn't stop hugging me. He just held me. A man just held me.

I was very uncomfortable with this long hug, but Jack wouldn't let me go. After about fifteen minutes, I finally started to relax and let my defenses down. The next thing I remember is being overwhelmed with this huge wave of emotion. Jack told me I didn't have to go anywhere.

He put his arm around my shoulder and we walked over to this bale of hay near the pond at Camp Marston. The tears began to flow, tears I'd been holding in about the loss of my mother, tears about the difficulty I was

47

having with it all. Pretty much 30 years' worth of tears.

Jack continued to listen. He didn't try to tell me that everything was going to be okay. He just spent time with me. It was the first time in my life that I allowed another man to be so close to me while my defenses were down like that.

It changed my life forever.

Brothering Spreads Universally

The toughest yet most satisfying vow of our earthly journey as men is the eternally evolving pledge to become brothers . . . eventually with the whole of Creation.

We start by paying holy tribute to those male ancestors in whose debt we stand and who are luring us forward: Kokopelli, the Native American humped-backed flute player; Orpheus, the father of music and poetry; Jesus of Nazareth, who incarnated the way of love; Francis of Assisi, a brother to the animals; John Sigismund, the first and only Unitarian monarch in history, whose ground-breaking edict established religious toleration and freedom; Unitarian Universalist Whitney Young, Jr., a persistent campaigner for racial justice; Mark DeWolfe, an openly gay Unitarian Universalist minister who, in the throes of dying with AIDS, wrote: "Remember your love as a source of strength; remember who you are: lovers tossed by these difficult times" . . . and countless other unsung brothers throughout history, pilgrims from the North and South, East and West.

Becoming brothers with a solitary man, then a few men, followed by more men, has a multiplying effect that fortifies us to become brothers with women and children as well. Authentic brothering becomes contagious, creating ever-widening circles of embrace . . . enfolding animals, stones, plants—creations related to yet quite distinct from humanoids. Brothering may also, certainly for some of us, produce linkage to infinite mysteries and powers beyond our comprehension, let alone our control . . . divine companions for the road.

This brothering adventure, this huge, foolish project that places us squarely in the lineage of Noah, is stunningly inclusive, beyond our wildest dreams, but it launches with those who share our genderal embodiment, with other men. It must start there, in accord with Walt Whitman's message that "all men are my brothers," not just the progressive, stimulating, agreeable ones of our choosing. Every man is our brother—including those men who frustrate, anger, even desert us; including those men who abuse, abandon, and kill women, children, and other men; including you yourself on your worst day; and, yes, including those guys who think that changing men's way of being in the world is irrelevant or worthless—all these men are our brothers too.

Brothering would re-member all men lest we inevitably dis-member. We salute men who are dead, living, yet to be born; men of all sexual orientations and celibates as well; men of every capacity, condition, color, class, and conviction; the athlete and the nurse; the outcast and the dictator; the hermit and the knight; the foe and the lover; the welder and the lawyer; leaders and followers and those who saunter to their own drumbeat; the honorable and the heinous, and an incorrigible mixture in us all; the magician and the impostor; the right-winger and the socialist.

We profoundly honor differences of color and ethnic heritage as gifts that contribute to a more resourceful brothering community. There is a special perspective obtained in being African-American, Latino, Asian, or Native, as well as Euro-American, in our Unitarian Universalist movement. We often ignore or forget the veritable richness in diversity. The blessings as well as the burdens of inclusion.

And certainly we are called to affirm, then serve, men who are numbered among the lost, the last, the least of society, in the respectful embrace of our ongoing Unitarian Universalist brotherhood. We would recall the judgment day parable in the Christian scriptures when Jesus pointedly says that if we've been serving the least of our brothers and sisters, we've been serving him.

If we've been clothing the naked, visiting prisoners, taking care of the wounded, the hungry, the homeless, the sick, then we've been displaying compassion not only to these folks (the bulk of whom are likely to be men) but also to Jesus and Buddha and Mohammed and Mother

Teresa as well. And, conversely, when we consistently fail to serve the least of these, our religion is fraudulent and futile.

I think of the man who, having just left prison, found a measure of restoration in our local men's fellowship. And the young adult who bravely described himself as "bedeviled with mental illness," crying out to our gathering of men: "Don't leave me out, don't leave me behind." It could have been our 42-year-old son, Chris, who is plagued with an emotional disorder that keeps him out of the flow of productive, mainline society, yet of whom his mother lovingly remarks: "Even the bird who cannot fly has a song." Yes, there must always be room in our brothering circles for all kinds of melodies, even dissonance.

But lest I romanticize matters, we aren't always successful. Men in recovery have fallen off the wagon while participating in our kinship; homeless men have tried our fellowship a few times, then wandered away, finding us too "stable" and "high-functioning." We started a group for battered and abused men, even one for male perpetrators of gender violence, and both of these circles enjoyed but a short lifespan on our liberal religious campus. You see, certain men are considered more audible and visible, that is, more spiritually acceptable, or plain comfortable, in our brothering circle than others are.

But Whitman's mission still obtains: All men are my brothers and to be treated as such.

We brothers remain an incorrigibly hopeful lot. Why? Because we belong to a life-affirming heritage. Because our redemptive religion makes us do it. We challenge Saddam Hussein and George Bush to spend an hour together, talking no politics, exchanging pictures of their grandchildren, making no demonizing references, being quiet for 10 straight minutes. Then placing their hands on each other's heart and taking turns, they would voice their deepest life-wounds and life-desires. If something even close to such intimacy could happen between Bush and Hussein, then these two demonized foes would be far less likely to ever harm the other, let alone do destructive things to other men, women, and children, over whom they hold massive sway.

Our ardent commitment to inclusive brothering reminds me of a Tolstoy story. One day the great Russian novelist was stopped by a street person who seemed weak, emaciated, and starving. Tolstoy searched his pockets for a coin but discovered that he was without a single penny. Taking the beggar's worn hands between his own, he said: "Don't be angry with me, my brother; I have nothing with me."

The lined face of the homeless man became illumined as he replied: "But you called me brother, you called me brother—which was gift enough!"

Yes, it is. Yes, it is.

Chapter 3: Toward a Mature Liberal Religious Masculinity

May I be accountable to my best self and my God!

—Lee Mun Wah

Our Unitarian Universalist faith offers a singular approach to deepening the reflective and prophetic lives of men. We're quite dissimilar from the evangelical Promise Keepers or the alternative "men's movements" circulating in the larger society. We're also different in content and manner from the smattering of mainline Protestant or Catholic, Jewish or Moslem men's programs. Not necessarily better, just distinct from these other growth options.

Hence, this chapter will attempt to delineate some of the salient features of a mature liberal religious masculinity.

Utterly Religious

Unitarian Universalists must create a real community for men rather than maintaining the institutional collective. We need a place where men are drawn in to share ourselves without fear of ridicule or rejection; a place where we're given the freedom to be understood rather than judged; a place where truth is replaced by meaning; a place where we can be unashamedly *religious.*

—Dick Michaels

From the beginnings of human life, men have congregated to hunt, to fight, to make plans, and to share meals. Sports teams, military squads, and brotherhoods of all configurations have formed as well—both within and without the church. In the last three decades, an embryonic men's movement has launched, flourished, then receded in prominence, with the bulk of its programming having transpired in the secular domain. Despite a strong undercurrent of spirituality, especially in the mythopoetic wing, men's work has rarely been institutionalized in religious form, except for the zealous outfit called *Promise Keepers*.

Nonetheless, it remains the belief of *Save the Males* that brothering is most fully realized in a spiritual setting. Religion combines its significance from the Latin words *re-ligare*, which translates as "binding again," and *re-legere*, which connotes "gathering together." Clearly, temples, sanghas, churches, and mosques are designated sites where women and men gather to bind themselves to the values and visions of their sacred traditions.

Through religious affiliation, brothers aspire to be securely bound *within* their own beings, bound *alongside* other like-minded men, bound *beyond* in benefit to society, and bound *through* kinship with the very cosmos itself. In truth, men's growth, when done well, balances the triune mandates of the full-service religious journey: personal renewal, social justice, and spiritual expansion. It grows men internally, externally, and eternally.

Consequently, houses of faith are the natural as well as optimal locales for serious, honorable pursuit of the deep masculine. The central charge of UUMeN—"nurturing a positive liberal religious masculinity"—summons Unitarian Universalist men to be a revolutionary force for abundant justice and joy starting within our chosen tribes.

Brothering is categorically a religious endeavor, since it prods men to address the primary questions of human existence: Who am I? What is my calling? Where am I going? Who will accompany me? What sustains me? And Whose am I? In religious homes, we answer these queries not alone but in community—being critiqued, challenged, and comforted through the embrace of kindred spirits.

In San Diego we've led *Brother-Spirit* sessions where the bi-focal needs of the masculine religious journey are addressed: brothering or *intimacy* and spirituality or *ultimacy*. We believe the religious life must always juggle reaching *within* through self-examination and meditative prayer, reaching *outside* in compassionate service and community-building, and reaching *beyond* to commune with the Infinite Spirit.

Other faith traditions have stepped up their own efforts to arrest men's flight from church involvement. Roman Catholic theologians have spawned a handful of books; so have Protestant and Jewish thinkers. The Presbyterian Church (U.S.A.) has even instituted an office that oversees the specific needs of men in their local parishes, with implications not only for programs, but also for liturgy, theology, and language.

The current emphasis of men's outreach, in most every religious communion, is more "support-focused" and less "project-oriented" than in the past. Furthermore, the rationale given for launching men's programming in other traditions rings familiar to our own ears: (1) When men are actively involved, the congregation thrives. (2) Spiritually nourished men become role models for others. (3) Men can lead the social ministry of the mosque, church, temple, or sangha in the larger world. (4) Men have unique concerns of their own to share and need stable and secure places to do so. (5) Men yearn for opportunities to grow and train for religious leadership.

But while we harbor much in common with other contemporary religious enterprises, we whittle our own pathway for men's soulful and prophetic growth. Ours would be a "mature liberal religious masculinity." What might that look like?

Unabashedly Liberal

The smudged yet noble watchword of our Unitarian Universalist faith heritage—*liberal*—has multiple meanings with relevance to the brothering revolution.

Unitarian Universalist men proudly claim to be liberal: receptive of mind, inclusive of spirit, generous of heart, and responsibly free of conscience—all bathed in a buoyant sense of hopefulness. We brashly contend that the world would be better off if more men embodied the liberal temper and spirit.

To be sure, brothers in the Unitarian Universalist fold often prefer alternative words to liberal such as progressive or freethinking, but sometimes we need to salvage and refurbish decent words. We must pour new wine into old wineskins. This may be the case with "liberal."

First, brothers are *open-minded*, not closed- or empty-minded. Revelation is not sealed and meaning has not been conclusively captured. Nothing is complete; thus everything and everyone is exposed to constructive criticism. This means that Unitarian Universalist men who are either ardent skeptics or believers must learn to work amicably, even productively, within the bosom of the same congregation. We need not only to tolerate but to welcome a wide range of political ideologies, theological opinions, and behavioral lifestyles in our brothering circles.

This imperative furnishes painful yet useful wisdom for any men who are set in our views and secure in our privileges. We belong to a movement marked by swinging doors and open windows. "Liberal" denotes that.

Of course, we hear the statement that "liberals never know what they believe." This reproach carries a gram of truth, for Unitarian Universalists don't know anything absolutely. But instead of taking this critique as a blow, let's receive it as a compliment. To know in part, to hold our operational wisdoms tentatively, means men are seriously engaging the complexities of reality rather than succumbing to slick dogmas.

The trouble with our world, according to Unitarian Universalist brothers, is that there are too many people who are too sure of too many things. *Liberal* religion is the opposite of *literal* religion. The mature masculine world requires ample freedom to believe and doubt, to affirm and protest, to agree and dissent.

Eschewing the extremes of utter sureness on the one hand and chaos on the other hand, Unitarian Universalist men proudly confess to being "card-carrying muddlers," who, according to Unitarian Universalist colleague Jack Mendelsohn, "live somewhere between the certainty that is repeatedly wrong and the uncertainty that leads to paralysis."

Second, being liberal means being *inclusive*, creating brothering tribes that are inviting to the WHAMMM majority within Unitarian Universalism but also embracing of brothers who represent different constituencies. Men's groups, in our Unitarian Universalist households, can devolve all too quickly into smug, homogenous clans.

Our American world remains loaded with male-dominated, nay, male-exclusive, organizations, some of which still only allow certain kinds of men into their membership, invariably WHAMMMers. It's the aspiration of authentically liberal brothering clans to stretch our imaginations and extend our arms—graduating from clubs, even coalitions, to genuine communities.

Men share the same gender embodiment; hence our histories are interlocking. This condition calls us to become inclusive, to welcome fresh and foreign brothers along our life-journey. As Parker Palmer notes: "Community is that place where the person you may least want to live with always lives!" Brothering demands such genuine community.

Third, being liberal means being *generous* of heart. The truly liberal man is magnanimous. His life is marked by open-handedness. He contributes freely and liberally, unstintingly of self and resources, energy and time. Grown-up men are not hoarders or simply takers. Brothers are givers and receivers in all zones of our lives: at work and play, home and church.

Fourth, liberal men are summoned to become *liberators*. Peter Maurin offers a pessimistic portrait of liberals as frozen in dispassionate mindsets:

> Liberals are often so liberal about everything that they
> refuse to be fanatical about anything . . . and not being
> fanatical about anything liberals cannot be liberators. They
> can only be liberals.

While I don't advocate fanaticism, I do exhort liberals to embody our sentiments. As bona fide liberals, brothers are more than freedom-seekers; we dare to be freedom-fighters on behalf of those who are enslaved, socially or spiritually. As Jack Mendelsohn pens: "The Latin word, *liber—*

from which both liberal and liberation spring—was the name of an ancient god of deliverance and growth. I believe in deliverance. I believe in growth." So do we on the brothering path in Unitarian Universalism.

There exists a demoralizing caricature of liberals as being those who have both feet firmly planted in the air. In actuality, the real liberal maintains that freedom is an instrumental value rather than an end in itself. As Martin Buber describes it, "Independence is a foot-bridge, not a dwelling-place. It's the run before the jump, the tuning of the violin. It's the possibility of communion."

Brothers aspire to become carriers of emancipation wherever bondage or servitude exists, be it men who are depressed, women who are oppressed, or children who are suppressed. As the Bible alerts us: "By their fruits shall ye know them!" The independent thoughts of brothers transform into responsibly freeing deeds.

Finally, the liberal man-ifesto denotes a chastened yet abiding *hopefulness*. A bedrock buoyancy. What does building a mature liberal religious masculinity mean? Our continental organization, UUMeN, answers thusly: "It means both honoring the goodness and courage in men as well as taking responsibility for the harm that we and our gender create."

Note the necessary balance. Without being blind to our male flaws, we don't believe that masculinity is an irredeemable estate. The brothering path is neither optimistic nor pessimistic, but hopeful. On the right sit reactionaries who disregard male privilege and ignore male-generated violence, arguing that men are as maltreated as women are, merely in different ways. In the opposing camp reside radicals who claim that masculinity constitutes a fatal condition, a hopeless cause.

UUMeN rejects such extremist postures in the name of equilibrium. On the one hand, we contend that male economic and political power are indeed privileged in contemporary culture, and on the other hand, we hold that men suffer greatly under the current social system. Perverted patriarchy cuts both ways, harms everyone. Consequently, we are called to be proud of being men but never at the expense of other men, women, or children.

When UUMeN purports to be a male-positive or male-enhancing organization, we are declaring that no matter what social travesties men perpetrate, ours can become a healthy and honorable station. The history of men is replete with both delivering and receiving wounds, but those wounds never exhaustively describe us.

We have been the beneficiaries of unearned entitlements; we can modify, even relinquish, those same benefits. We have stuffed our emotions and stunted our souls; but we can reform. We have learned racist behaviors; nonetheless, we can unlearn them. Bottom line: men can change. It will prove a lifelong, rugged endeavor, but men can change.

We are hopeful about the male gender. We believe that men can repent, resist, reconcile, and rejoice . . . trekking toward the full manhood for which we were created.

The Promise Keepers and the Progress Keepers

This is a challenging time to sustain a brothering presence, since the initial popularity of men's programming in American culture has been waning. Except for some fine outreach by the New Warriors (now known as *The Mankind Project*) and occasional men's gatherings with Robert Bly, Michael Meade, Martin Prechtel, James Hillman and sundry cohorts, the only burgeoning alternative on the scene appears to be the religious right's option called *Promise Keepers*.

Our UUMeN's approach, while admiring certain elements of these secular and fundamentalist male endeavors, furnishes a clear alternative to both. Kenneth Beldon likes to think of UUMeN as being *progress* keepers. I have no quarrel with his amendment; I only pray that such a title proves accurate in our local congregations, where brothering challenges are fired and tested.

Promise Keepers in its heyday in the mid-1990s was replete with a $100 million budget and a staff of 400, plus a slick magazine, *New Man*. On the other hand, our UUMeN organization is without any paid staff person and still scrambling for sufficient membership and funding as we celebrate our 10th anniversary in 2003.

However, Promise Keepers is now scrambling too and has made sizable cutbacks. Just a few years ago, 280,000 evangelical men packed seven football stadiums glorifying God, slapping "high-fives," and pompously greeting one another with "Thank God, you're a man." Their uncompromising objective remains to "take the nation for Jesus Christ."

It's worth doing a modest exegesis of the tenets of Promise Keepers, since UUMeN offers a strikingly distinct version of masculine spirituality. In noting consequential differences in the three areas of sexual orientation, gender, and racial justice, our own liberal religious agenda for men will be clarified.

Sexual Orientation Justice

Almost as a foundational principle, Promise Keepers refers to gays as "stark raving mad . . . an abomination against Almighty God." Or "homosexuals are a group of people who don't reproduce yet want to be compared to people who do." On the contrary, Unitarian Universalist men are fearless pacesetters, progress-keepers, if you will, in the drive for the full dignity of lesbians, gays, bisexual, and transgender people, although the dehumanizing monsters of heterosexism and homophobia have yet to be eradicated from our own liberal nest.

Does society realize the crushing devastation to the souls and bodies of gay youth who are trapped in an ever-downward spiral of shame as they struggle with the same need every male has for tenderness and love? In *What the Bible Really Says about Homosexuality* (1994), Daniel Helminiak recounts two tragic results of societal intolerance of gay youth: (1) 30–40% of children living on the streets have been thrown out or left their homes because they are gay; (2) 30% of teenage suicides are among gay youth—a rate two to three times higher than the national norm.

Issues of erotic preference especially cause men to squirm, to become defensive and rigid, often lashing out belligerently, even destructively, as in the case of Matthew Shepard's killing. Conversely, when gay, straight, bisexual, and transgender men risk moving from closets to closeness, speaking our deepest truths, venturing beneath surfaces, beyond expectations, and beside prejudices, the results can be utterly transformative.

But don't be lulled. We live in a culture that is both homophobic and philiaphobic, and this double-whammy renders male intimacy a rare accomplishment, even in our Unitarian Universalist fold. So the task of growing affectional honesty, let alone friendship, across sexual orientation lines, continues to constitute a revolutionary adventure.

Gender Justice

Promise Keepers also defends the primacy of the male in the household and unapologetically commands members to "take back the reins of spiritually pure leadership God intended men to hold." One of their pastoral leaders, Tony Evans, upon instructing husbands how to recover their manhood, declares: "The first thing you do is sit down with your wife and say: 'Honey, I made a terrible mistake. I gave you my role. I gave up leading this family, and I forced you to take my place. Now I must reclaim that role.'"

He goes on: "Don't misunderstand me, men. I'm not suggesting that you *ask* for your role back, I'm urging you to *take* it back. . . . Be sensitive. Listen. Treat the lady gently and lovingly. But LEAD!" As an outgrowth of their sexist posture, Promise Keepers targets "sissified men" as the main cultural problem in America.

Promise Keepers assumes the only thing required to improve women's lives is for men to seize the reins. They contend that patriarchal power is legitimate and, in fact, desirable, so long as it is not "misused" and the patriarchs practice benevolent domination.

As another Promise Keepers leader put it, "Man is the head of the household and women are responders. God's revelation comes through man not woman, so the two genders can never be equal." The women's auxiliary organization is aptly called "Suitable Helpers."

A pertinent concern relates to women's reproductive health and rights. While moral convictions about abortion vary across all religious persuasions, those of us partial to mature liberal religious masculinity suggest that men's movements ought to be dedicated to male responsibility in preventing unintended pregnancies. Abortion rates would drop dramatically, if men simply refused to have unprotected intercourse unless we're willing to be devoted, supportive, lifelong fathers.

Unitarian Universalist brothers oppose male supremacy and female subordination in our culture, in whatever guise, and labor steadfastly for

61

gender fairness socially, politically, physically, economically, familially, and spiritually. It's critical that men play a staunch, sympathetic role in women's struggle for equality. The health and welfare of our mutual destinies are interwoven.

Gloria Steinem puts it compellingly:

> After all, if it's fair to say that there is more virtue where there is more choice, then men who choose to reject male privilege may be more virtuous than the rest of us. They will earn our trust. They will also discover the full circle of human qualities within themselves. The truth is this: for both women and men, completing our full circle lies in the direction we have not been.

As men we will never discover full humanity solely by reclaiming our emotions, connecting with brothers, and making peace with our fathers. The way to wholly restore our lost masculinity and to heal the fractured earth is through toiling for a scope of revolutionary justice that serves the disenfranchised of our globe: women and children; persons of color; gays and lesbians, bisexuals and transgender folks; the physically and emotionally disabled; the homeless, the incarcerated, the marginalized.

The Challenge of Being Pro-Feminist Men

> Pro-feminism is very male-affirmative because it affirms men shedding their violent ways and becoming more whole, caring men.
>
> —Andrea Dworkin

I often hear Unitarian Universalist male comrades saying, "I don't have the energy or time to be political. I'm hurting too much myself." I offer two plain responses.

First, I enduringly care about the personal plight of my brothers and energetically invite any men in need to join a support group. In San Diego we've sustained upwards of 15 active men's kinship circles. I've personal-ly belonged to one for 18 years. So I attend deeply to the sizable hurts and hungers of men, including my own.

I understand, even applaud, the process of men venting long-fester-ing agonies and woes. Wounded animals are the most dangerous, and mature men must aggressively face our injuries on the path toward heal-ing. But being wounded is only part of our story. We men are also wounders, and we must answer for that. We need to heed the unbearable pain and terror that women and children feel, living in a world in which one in four women will be raped and one in six children is the victim of sexual abuse.

Second, since we're incorrigibly social animals, we men can ill afford to smugly gaze at our navels without being public contributors. Mature masculinity and our brand of religion require that we heal both the body personal and the body politic.

Feminism reminds men that women's rights and concerns have not been satisfactorily addressed yet and that sexism has not been con-quered—yea, even in our liberal Unitarian Universalist fold. Several years ago our Beacon Press published a trenchant volume entitled *Against the Tide: Pro-Feminist Men in the United States, 1776–1990 (A Documentary History)*, edited by Michael S. Kimmel and Thomas E. Mosmiller. It remains a timely book that belongs in the library of every Unitarian Universalist pilgrim dedicated to creating gender justice and joy in our religious association and the larger world.

The authors, whom I've met through our common participation in the National Organization of Men Against Sexism (NOMAS), are not detached social analysts but committed pro-feminist brothers. They're active contributors in both word and deed in diminishing gender injus-tice. When launching this six-year project in quest of "men who sup-ported feminism," they were chided, "Well, that'll be the shortest book in history!"

Much to everyone's astonishment, the search unearthed over 1000 documents, 135 of which are presented in the book, attesting to men's support throughout American history for women's equality. The state-ments are crisply excerpted and organized under the rubrics of the pre–Seneca Falls era and the struggles for equal education, economic, political and social equality, concluding with a revealing section on "contemporary pro-feminist men." Intentional effort is made to include gays as well as men of color, men from diverse economic and vocational backgrounds, conservatives as well as card-carrying progressives, famous men and unsung advocates, too.

One of the most stirring essays is that of the abolitionist Frederick Douglass, who resolutely linked the anti-slavery and pro-suffrage causes. "Woman," he wrote, "cannot be elevated without elevating man, and man cannot be depressed without depressing woman also."

The only arena unaddressed in this book is women's quest for religious equality, which is surprising since so many of the pro-feminist men represented in this collection are spiritual leaders and clergy, including about ten Unitarians and Universalists.

The authors clarify that in the struggle for women's equality, pro-feminist men have provided support, not leadership. They've labored in the background rather than paraded in the foreground. Occasionally men have paid the price of derision, even vilification, for opposing male supremacy and female subordination.

In truth, many of American history's pro-feminist men were reluctant reformers, displaying periodic ambivalence and inconsistency, failing to match their public pronouncements with private behaviors—advocating, for example, equal education while opposing suffrage. They were men of their times, justice-builders whose records on behalf of women's equality were flawed. Yet all remained steadfast for the transcendent cause, standing behind and alongside their sisters.

The pro-feminism articulated in *Against the Tide* falls into three main categories: men supporting women's equality because it was right and just; because women were believed to embody a superior morality; and because feminist gains generated benefits for men as well.

The authors judiciously label these exemplars pro-feminist because "they *believed* in feminism. But to *be* a feminist requires another ingredient: the felt experience of oppression. And this men cannot feel because men are not oppressed but privileged by sexism." I also prefer the term pro-feminist to anti-sexist, because it's strikingly affirmative.

This splendid book records an undeniable, oft-forgotten strain in United States history of men boldly witnessing to gender justice. As long as women have valiantly pursued equality in this land, against continuing resistance, there have also existed male companions in the struggle. The tide has been met, if not stemmed, by these pro-feminist brothers and the sisters whose quest they've undergirded.

UUMeN has joined this illustrious, living tradition of pro-feminist brothers. It explicitly urges contemporary men to be pro-feminist supporters up close with the partners, mothers, daughters, and other women who share our personal and professional lives, recognizing that gender justice that is practiced publicly but not privately is fraudulent.

Privilege, while granting men power, causes costly, irreparable damage to our own bodies and souls. It's an undeniable lesson of our Unitarian Universalist brothering revolution that feminism lies in men's deeper interests. Working as allies with women to make the ideals of equality substantive is integral to the fullest expression of what it means to be brothers.

Both genders have much work to do, for we've still not approximated the mid-19th century exhortation of our Unitarian foresister Margaret Fuller: "A new manifestation is at hand, a new hour is come, when Man and Woman may regard one another as brother and sister, able both to appreciate and to prophesy to one another."

Racial Justice

Promise Keepers also boldly invites racial reunion, yet with sweet and inoffensive riffs, never even mentioning systemic racism. Persons of various colors joining hands in song or testimony, even apology, is important but insufficient work. Institutional racism may be momentarily soothed, but never permanently tackled, merely with caring embraces.

However, as Unitarian Universalists know, our own movement possesses a checkered record in confronting the overt and covert racism both within and beyond our walls. There's probably no more cantankerous sin for Unitarian Universalists to confess and combat, not as a three-year task force but as a lifetime effort, than racism. Deep is our liberal denial of the intransigent racism that permeates Unitarian Universalist culture and results in paralyzing guilt or resignation, rather than heartfelt repentance followed by substantive change.

Repentance is a key concept in anti-racism work, because it denotes our persistent willingness not to turn away or turn against but to "turn around"—to change wrongful ways. Repentance means blowing the whistle on the blatant as well as the small, disguised, unintentional assaultive acts white men, individually and collectively, perpetrate against persons of color. It means making right what has been wrong. Authentic remorse results in both attitudinal adjustment and behavioral change.

Racism is primarily a white responsibility, and we men must battle it in our souls as well as carry our load in its institutional elimination. However, liberal religious folks, men as well as women, are often more enamored with maintaining a positive self-image or looking good to the outside world than dedicated to opposing the demon of racism itself. Yet being an agent of revolutionary justice must transcend being cloyingly polite or politically correct. It means pursuing the path of prophetic compassion in a society that increasingly undermines racial and gender affirmative action.

White folks are doing all they can to keep tight control of my home state of California, precisely when minorities are rising to power in numbers and the demand for equity. Where will Unitarian Universalist brothers stand as matters heat up, as lines are drawn, and as the culture clash intensifies across the continent? What will we say and do when the forces of intolerance, bigotry, and exclusion grow more intractable in the outside world and subtler within our own religious walls? Will we stand tall for justice as Unitarian Universalist men or will we step down, back off, and sneak away to another more fashionable social cause?

I personally identify with the way white activist Robert Terry phrases the challenge: "I'm not offended if you call me a racist but am if that's all you call me!" In fostering a mature liberal religious masculinity, we aspire to be anti-racist racists!

To conclude, when Promise Keepers talks about "privilege," they aren't referring to unearned male entitlements in modern society, they are talking instead about the privilege of knowing Jesus.

66

Well, their promises and ours are markedly different, and while these fundamentalist men are ardently trying to regain male supremacy in western culture, our UU Men's Network aspires to forge a more just and merciful reality. A clash of religious worldviews prevails in our world, and ready or not, the men and women of our Unitarian Universalist faith must rise up and be counted for the equitable, compassionate, life-affirming sacred path.

Eight Vows of Mature Liberal Religious Men

Nonetheless, Promise Keepers and UUMeN share the conviction that for men to change, we must make and keep our commitments. Vows are solemn pledges by which we bind ourselves to certain acts. Unitarian Universalism is a covenantal, not a creedal, faith and, as such, based not on right beliefs but on enduring promises. Ours is a vow-making religion.

As Lewis Smedes puts it: "When we make a promise, we control at least one thing. We will be there no matter what the circumstances are." In our religious faith, being liberal has too frequently been mis-equated with being footloose and fancy-free—committed only so long as we feel like it.

On the contrary, Unitarian Universalists choose neither bondage nor bondlessness but healthy, holy bonds. To contribute to a saner and more respectful universe, men must do our fair share in enfleshing vows that major in results, not rhetoric. As our Unitarian forebrother Horace Mann urged: "Be ashamed to die until you have won some victory for humanity."

Men need to grow adept at pledging our full *troth* to building a more just and joyful world. While a bit quaint, troth is a splendid word that combines both *truthfulness* and *trust*. Truthfulness means men will intentionally spread no lies. And trust means we will commit no deliberate harm unto one another. Brenda Ueland claims that compassionate community entails two major virtues: "No lying and no cruelty!" We on the brothering path heartily agree.

If UUMeN were to generate eight key vows that mature liberal religious men are advised to sustain in order to become soulful and prophetic brothers, the list might resemble the following.

Vow 1: Live **RELATIONALLY**

A foundational vow is for men to live *relationally*, not independently. Lone-rangerism is a damaging malaise, learned from boyhood on. We are men by birth, but we become brothers through an intentional effort to relate caringly and justly to other living entities—starting with other men, often the hardest relational challenge for males.

Our liberal religious heritage has venerated rugged individualists such as Henry David Thoreau while underrating institutionalists like Henry Whitney Bellows. We've well nigh forgotten those distinguished Universalist men who formed spiritual-prophetic brotherhoods such as the Hopedale Community and the Humiliati. We proclaim the interdependent web as an ecological and cosmic principle, as well we should, but we frequently fail to embody it in the smaller kinship groups where we dwell. Men remain gravely underdeveloped in the craft of relational power.

Consequently, the governing mandate of our Unitarian Universalist Men's Network has been to establish an intentional community of brothers and sister-allies committed, as our bylaws put it, "to building a positive liberal religious masculinity that is pro-feminist, gay-affirmative, culturally and racially inclusive and diverse. We understand such positive masculinity, working in alliance with various movements for social justice, as essential for personal and social progress, healthy spirituality, and the good life." Right off the bat, our Unitarian Universalist brothering revolution saw the absolute necessity of "working in alliance" with others, that is, operating relationally.

UUMeN forces us to admit that we're not self-sufficient, either as individual males or as autonomous brotherhoods. UUMeN is at heart a shared ministry by, for, and to men. And we cherish women standing alongside, rooting men on, even as they need us to return the favor on their gender quest.

When men risk living relationally—trading in patterns of aloofness, alienation, and abuse for bonds of affirmation and affection—then we'll bring an astounding wealth of inner resources to the table with other men, women, children, earth, and deities.

Brothering is a direct validation of the relational principles of Unitarian Universalism.

Vow 2: Be RESPONSIBLE

Being accountable means playing neither ignorant nor inadequate, but utilizing whatever power we males possess, both individually and collectively, to alter the world. In our UUA Principles and Purposes, responsibility has a high priority, being referenced twice: we affirm "the free and responsible search for truth and meaning" and we are called to "respond to God's love by loving our neighbors as ourselves."

Responsible men redress our wrongs rather than ignoring or wallowing in them. Brothers dare to approach another man, woman, or child and apologize for how we may have mistreated them: to make amends; to restore, if possible, any outstanding tormented or devastated bonds.

The truth is that no viable, lasting solution to a relational crisis is found by blaming others, only by calling one's self to accountability. As men we must, first and foremost, take care of "our own side of the street."

But there's more to address. Responsible men not only aspire to mend brokenness with other individuals but also with those institutions we've ignored or aggrieved. Reconciliation is often construed as merely a personal matter, but it's markedly more. In combating any injustice, we must atone with specific sisters and brothers as well as confront underlying, transgenerational, and systemic wrongs.

In his courageous book *Healing Violent Men: A Model for Christian Communities,* David Livingston draws a cogent distinction:

> Reconciliation is distinct from forgiveness and is a communal rather than an individual phenomenon. Reconciliation has its linguistic roots in re-conciliation, that is, rejoining the concilium or community. This aspect of rejoining the community is distinct from reunion, which is merely re-uniting something that was once a unity. Reconciliation must address healing in the individ-

69

ual sphere, the interhuman sphere, and the social sphere. It is only through accountability on all three levels of relationship that a transformation to a nonviolent society is possible.

Men are challenged to be fully responsible in all spheres of existence. However, too many members of WHAMMM (white, heterosexual Anglo-Saxon, middle-class, middle-aged males) languish in self-pity because we're seemingly targeted as the Pharaoh in everyone else's Exodus effort. In truth, WHAMMMers have three basic options: (1) self-denial, where I continue to benefit as a dominator; (2) self-commiseration, where I moan and snivel; or (3) self-fulfillment, where I confess my culpability without succumbing to guilt, then proceed as an ally for justice and joy.

The question remains for a still predominantly WHAMMM-run enterprise such as Unitarian Universalism: Will we be motivated to continue or arrest our domination? Will we exhibit foot-dragging and backlash or demonstrate sincere repentance?

Repentance doesn't mean breast-beating. It means, in the parlance of 12-step groups, to take a courageous moral inventory—then to apologize and to deliver compensation. Repentance calls men to halt what we're doing, change directions, make restitution, and get back on course.

I implore my fellow brothers to quit blaming other men or women and cease banking on any deities to accomplish what we must and can do ourselves. Reconcile, repent, and be responsible.

I've discovered in my brothering circles over the past 30 years that men actually want to be held responsible for what we do with who we are and what we possess. Unitarian Universalist minister Peter Fleck recalls seeing a drama on television in which a man dies and finds himself standing in line, addressed by a nonchalant usher who tells him he can choose either door, the one on the right leading to heaven, or the one on the left leading to hell.

"You mean I can choose either one?" the man asks. "There's no judgment, no taking account of how I've lived?"

"That's right," the usher says. "Now move along, people are dying and lining up behind you. Choose one door and keep the line moving."

"But I want to confess, I want to come clean, I want to be judged."
"We don't have time for that. Just choose a door and move along."
The man walks through the door on the left, leading to hell.

Fleck's conclusion is that, in the end, we want to be held accountable. We want to be judged for the character and conduct of our lives, and, ultimately, to be forgiven as well.

Vow 3: REJOICE in Our Own Gender

Men must learn to *rejoice* in our own gender but never at the price of others. I say learn, because so many men possess a highly-honed negative self-image, no matter how self-assured, even pompous, we may appear in public. We would also delight in our own peculiar embodiment of maleness, but never in comparison to another brother. Rejoicing is grounded in authentic, earned pride, not arrogance.

Therefore, we don't tolerate the bashing of women, gays, lesbians, bisexuals, transgender persons or persons of color, and we refuse as well to scorn or humiliate men *qua* men. Mature men want our individual selves as well as our entire gender to be celebrated without being idolized, to be challenged without being trivialized.

Joy—deeper than happiness and more enduring than pleasure—is central to any brothering path. You've probably heard about the bishop who lamented: "Wherever Jesus went, there was a revolution; wherever I go, people serve tea!" Well, that's but a partial truth, for, in fact, Jesus was both a partygoer and a prophetic force. And while the Nazarene didn't attend tea parties, he did gravitate to wine feasts.

Even one of our premier workhorses for justice, Theodore Parker, noted the glaring absence of exuberance among his mid–19th-century Unitarian colleagues:

> Most powerfully preaching to the conscience and the will,
> the cry was ever "duty, duty! work, work!" They failed to
> address with equal power the spirit, and did not also shout
> "joy, joy! delight, delight!" Their vessels were full of water,
> but they did not gush out, leaping from the great spring. . . .

Indeed, our brothering quest is joy-filled. It hankers for an abundance of laughers, singers, clowns, and dancers among its revolutionary company. To keep men off-balance, Robert Bly often remarks at the beginning of a conference: "Today we'll say a few things that are true, but we don't know which ones they are!" Such self-humor keeps brothers relaxed and matters flowing. Music generates merriment as well, lest we take ourselves too seriously. As the African saying goes: "Bad people have no song."

Vow 4: Be RECREATIVE of Body

> When I sense the holiness of my own body, I begin to sense the holiness of every other body.
>
> —James Nelson

Brothers aspire to be *recreative* of body. Integral to re-creation is becoming playful beings: playful not for triumph, although competitive push-and-pull can prove growthful, but primarily for the sake of bouncing and sweating, moving and leaping, chanting and drumming. Men need to engage in frisky, gleeful activities where we recreate more for renewal than for reward—being the animals we truly are.

As Robert Fulghum reminds us, "To be a useful Hopi is to be one who has a quiet heart and takes part in all the dances." Dancing has never hurt either the ground or anyone else, and men sorely need to learn how to touch others and the earth for delight, not for harm.

Upon returning from their solitary exploits, the 12th-century Knights Templars would seek communion not through talk, though there were many spirited tales to be told, but through dance. With their arms clasped in a circle and their bodies moving in unison on the earth, they received one another through dance. No wonder we're called a men's movement, not a men's system!

Vow 5: RELEASE Our Hearts

For men to shape an evolving brotherhood, we pledge to *release* our hearts from emotional miserliness. It's no secret that men are socialized to live emotionally constricted, physically shortened, spiritually blocked lives. Whole men are both pale-blooded (reflective and sweet) and red-blooded (fiery and assertive) and exude such expansive emotionality on a daily basis. As my buddy in the movement puts it, "I wish all brothers both bubbles and lightning!" Hence, mature men exhibit testosterone-with-heart.

One of the most prevalent yet almost completely ignored disorders in modern society is male depression. It remains unmanly and shameful for men to admit their despondency, let alone seek help. Yet the high price men pay for withholding our feelings of hurt and anger can include sleeping disorders, irritability, indecisiveness, a sense of worthlessness, recurrent thoughts of death, and clinical depression.

Conversely, when men risk sharing feelings of rage, fright, and mourning (the threesome I delineate as anger, angst, and anguish)—whenever we open ourselves up in faithful intimacy with men—we're never able to close up as tightly again. Mature liberal religious men are starting to recognize that the best antidote to depression is not medication, essential as that can be, but verbal revelation and tearful release.

Native Americans say spirituality means possessing a moist heart, because the soil of the human heart is necessarily watered with tears that keep the ground soft. And from such turf new life is born.

Tears of joy, sadness, and gratitude furnish one profound gauge of a man becoming a brother. We must open the tear ducts and allow our crying to fertilize the earth. As novelist Pat Conroy put it:

> I could feel the tears within me, undiscovered and untouched in their inland sea. Those tears had been with me always. I thought that, at birth, American men are allotted just as many tears as American women are. But because we are forbidden to shed them, we die long before women die, our hearts exploding or our blood pressure rising or our livers eaten away by alcohol because

that lake of grief inside us has no outlet. We men die because our faces are not watered enough.

Vow 6: RESTORE Our Souls

Men typically spend our days climbing over our fellow human beings or climbing up all sorts of mountains yet fail to recharge our batteries via quietude and rest. Brother David Steindl-Rast warns, "the Chinese pictograph for *busy* is composed of two characters: 'heart' and 'killing.'"

We are driven to do and to have, but we have forgotten to *be*. Men revise our own beings as well as the greater world, whenever we decide to *restore* our harried, thin souls with intentional times of Sabbath and self-care. That's why we call our San Diego weekend get-aways for men "renewals." They're deliberate respites geared to replenish our beings.

Adult males possess few clues about how to surrender to the yearnings of our hearts, the flow of an unscheduled day, the caress of our partner, the invitation of the Divine. This lack is glaringly evident among goal-oriented, productive Unitarian Universalist types.

In order to be mature male beings, we should practice the unaccompanied art of reflection, being still without having to acquire or achieve anything. When men spend at least 15 minutes a day in restorative silence or prayerful contemplation, we become less frenzied, more serene and centered. Better professionals, partners, and parents too.

Vow 7: Bridge with RESPECT

Mature men vow to build the bridge called *respect* with the entire universe, starting with our human brothers and sisters: pledging to disarm our souls in their presence, to share our truths with growing trust. Right relationship is the phrase the Buddhists use to describe being in just and caring connection with all living reality. It entails deliberately pursuing intergender understanding and equity, companioning children in kindly ways, being stewards (husbandmen) of the earth's resources, growing in reverential communion with the Eternal Spirit.

Vow 8: Undertake a REVOLUTION

Any brimming enthusiasm in the larger culture for men's work and growth has died down. Men's retreats in the woods are less frequent. Robert Bly has returned to his principal passion: composing poetry. There used to be numerous gender studies departments in universities that specifically addressed issues of masculinity—not so anymore. Nowadays you can rarely find a shelf in bookstores specifically on men's growth. Our concerns, if addressed at all, are hidden in the sections on women or sexual orientation.

For many, the men's movement is now perceived as a passing fancy, essentially kaput. That's all the more reason for local brothering circles to deem ourselves not as a short-term fix but as a presence. We need to keep on keeping on as long as men walk the earth.

Authentic brothering marks not merely a corrective measure but a revolutionary endeavor. Changing men changing the world causes radical, ongoing repercussions. When men become brothers, all our bonds are altered, our work and family lives are enriched (even if initially destabilized), and our drives to repair society and heal the cosmos are rendered more urgent. And remember: any robust revolution worth pursuing is both personal and global—it changes the heart while contributing gifts back to the universe as well. A revolution has internal, external, and eternal ramifications; otherwise, it will play partial, or false.

But why call this summons to brothering a revolution? Because UUMeN contends that contemporary times require more than new information or the gradual reformation of attitude. The 21st century demands the full-fledged transformation of being, wherein our male lives are turned both outside-in (reflectively) and inside-out (prophetically).

The brothering imperative reminds men that, with grace and grit, the perils and tyrannies pervading our lives can be diminished. Furthermore, men, both individually and organizationally, must take the lead in our own overhaul. The membership of the continental UUMeN is not interested in the evolution of male consciousness so much as the revolution of male conduct. As Unitarian Universalist compadre Albert Schweitzer exclaimed, "My life—my argument!"

75

The word revolution comes from a Latin word denoting "to roll back" or "to unroll." Consequently, the unclouded purpose of brothering is to roll back the assumptions, biases, and behaviors that suppress men's psyches, oppress women socially and economically, and wreak ecological havoc. Rolling back the negatives so positives might be unrolled is the delightful duty of practicing revolutionaries committed to growing a mature liberal religious masculinity.

I appreciate the way Kate Millett phrased it in her groundbreaking book entitled *Sexual Politics* (1970): "Guys still have it in their heads that a revolutionary is a murderer. Uh-uh. A revolutionary is a changer, a teacher, somebody who hangs in and keeps at it, and keeps loving people until they change their heads." And I would amend: until they change their hearts and souls as well.

Life is a partisan fray, and the tests and tribulations facing men are colossal. To confront our own stubborn aches and buried wounds will require revolutionary honesty. To modify the course of our chosen faith-tradition will require revolutionary defiance. To cultivate spiritual terrain while navigating political waters will require revolutionary balance. To stop the emotional and physical harm we daily perpetrate on women, children, other men, and ourselves will require revolutionary courage. To bridge the power gap between WHAMMMers and non-WHAMMMers will require revolutionary chutzpah.

Launching the continental UUMeN a decade ago in 1993, specifically to challenge the privileged status of our own gender, took what writer Toni Cade Bambara terms "sheer holy boldness." In the annals of human history, it's quite unusual for men, basking in entitlements, to promote and affirm brotherhoods that call for men to change: in effect, to jettison rather than fortify our empires. Yet we assert that now's the time for WHAMMMers—still the most empowered group of human beings that ever inhabited the planet—to rise from our seats of privilege and to commit a revolutionary deed: to extend the realm of justice to enfold every living reality.

A Hasidic tale underscores the primacy of our male accountability. When Rabbi Ammi's hour to die came, he wept bitterly, not because he wasn't a thoughtful gentleman or a learned scholar of the sacred Torah, but because Ammi failed to become a public servant. He wept because, as he put it, "I was given the ability to extend justice, but never carried it out." If UUMeN progressively embraces rather than evades our founding mission, we will become imperfect yet persistent justice-builders and joy-bringers.

To evolve from being males, our biological fate, to brothers, our relational destiny, requires revolutionary strides. Being a brother to other men and women, to plants and animals, to the deities and demons roaming the universe signals nothing less than a revolutionary passage from dominator to collaborator. The revolution we're trying to sustain demands extraordinary masculine fortitude and, yes, will extract a substantial cost. And while I'm not optimistic about our common tomorrows, I remain uncompromisingly hopeful.

As this new millennium advances, we are shamelessly agitating for every registered Unitarian Universalist man and supportive sister-ally to join our revolutionary voyage. The bylaws of the UUMeN are unavoidably clear: we "challenge men to confront gender injustice, homophobia, racism, loneliness and distrust between men, and violence by men against women, children, other men, themselves, and the earth." And to do so at our places of residence, work, play, and worship.

However, as Thomas Sankara said during his presidency of the West African country of Burkina Faso, "You can't make fundamental changes in society without the occasional mad act."

The mad act could mean confronting gay-baiting or lesbian-bashing humor on our jobs. It could mean caring for a child so an overworked single mother can have a day that is her own. It could mean being willing not only to assist women caught in harm's way, but also to applaud women in times of their power and glory. It could mean refusing to hold a men's retreat until the active presence and gifts of blue-collar men and men of color are included.

It could mean working to heal male victimizers: men who batter other men or women, men who are prison rapists, men who are child molesters, men who are murderers. And if these brothers can't be healed, then laboring to place them securely back in institutions and to keep advocating whatever rehabilitation might be possible.

And the mad act could mean becoming a true husbandman: prudently conserving the earth's resources, cultivating the soil, and exhibiting kinship toward plants and animals.

Unitarian Universalists are notorious for feverishly passing resolutions in favor of changing institutions in the outside world, while failing to modify the unjust policies and deeds of our own religious clan. In the recent efforts to grow an anti-racist, multi-cultural religious movement in the UUA, we've had to look squarely at the nagging inequities that riddle our own household rather than simply addressing societal damage.

So don't expect the revolution of true brothering to be either effortless or pleasant. We're still, for the most part, a male-entrenched and controlled operation, and manifold men—as well as some women—won't readily modify the comfortable arrangement in our Association from which so many of us gain considerable and unquestioned benefit.

Revolutionary religious experiments that exemplify what Unitarian forebrother Roger Baldwin called "holy discontent" are seldom popular or centrist. Avowed Unitarian Universalist brothers must persist and plod, remaining true to our purpose, marked by what Gloria Steinem calls "outrageous acts and everyday rebellions."

Liberal religious men confess that life's infirmities and inequities will not be eradicated during our lifetimes. Nonetheless, we aspire to be consistently conscious even when we're not always just. And we cannot hold to optimism, but neither are we cynics who futilely throw in the towel. As Unitarian Universalists, we remain inveterate hopers who know that, on occasion, our faulty revolutionary talk and walk may just, as the Hopis say, grow some corn.

Chapter 4: Joining Ethics and Power

The planet needs warriors and men of conscience. In the current state of affairs we have too many powerful men without ethics and ethical men without power. We need to teach the powerful to have ethics. And the ethical men must learn how to become powerful.

—Aaron Kipnis

You're probably wondering why this sweet, agreeable guy is tackling such politically-charged topics as men and power, men and violence, and men and aging. I'm wondering myself.

Yet, in truth, I know why. Basically, I'm trying to be morally braver during my homestretch. I'm also set on pushing my own gender toward greater accountability. If we're ever going to approximate a more mature liberal religious masculinity in the 21st century, men can't just massage our navels and purge our souls. We can't merely feel good; we've got to try to be good and do well, and that requires full engagement with the most difficult and demanding of ethical quandaries.

The Basic Meaning of Power

Power is the formative factor directing our daily lives, more so than love, deep dreams and passions of the soul, or the advances of technology.

—James Hillman

The essential definition of power, rather innocent on its own, is the agency to act, derived from the Latin *posse*, "to be able." Some modicum of power comes with the territory of being alive. Power, *per se*, is amoral. It may be rational or irrational, constructive or destructive in its consequences.

When Nietszche proclaimed, "Wherever I found the living, there I found the will to power," he was implying that we fulfill ourselves through demonstrating our able-ness, through wielding the might with which we've been blessed. That some humans have been robbed of our bedrock dignity or that others of us have squandered our strength doesn't diminish the fact that being powerful is an original blessing shared in common.

Power is the application of mind and courage to force. When unreleased or squashed, power dissipates, and human beings wither. To actualize our god-given power, then, is the basic charge delivered at birth. As Emerson said: "Do the thing and you shall have the power. But they who do not the thing, have not the power." Therefore, the gravest human tragedy is not that we die, but that we fail to employ our full capacity while we're alive.

We earthlings fabricate all sorts of reasons for not using our power: we are cursed by defective genes or a dysfunctional upbringing, or bedeviled by an avalanche of adult crises, or ravaged by outright oppression. But accurate explanations don't produce adequate excuses. The fact remains that numerous sisters and brothers who have suffered deep and wide gashes, not of their own making, are still stirred to live as empowered and empowering human beings.

Men Are Powerful

Modern men are ensnared amidst a contradiction. On the one hand, adult males possess considerable societal power, yet, much of the time, they feel personally powerless. How come? This dilemma needs to be addressed.

All economic, social, and political indicators verify that men hold more power than women do. Despite complaints of reverse discrimination, according to the data, white males account for 32.9% of the population but 82.5% of the Forbes 400, 70% of tenured college faculty, and, after the 1994 elections, 79% of that Congress.

Money plays a major role in power disparities in our culture. As James Hillman writes: "The Economy determines who is included and who is marginalized, distributes the rewards and punishments of wealth and poverty, advantage and disadvantage." Economic power is thus linked with political power, which is built on physical power, which is ultimately the power of violence or its threat. And WHAMMMers clearly enjoy the bulk of material wealth in the world.

Indeed, economic privilege is among the subtlest and most damaging of the WHAMMM factors. That's why current UUA President Bill Sinkford perceptively notes: "We're about to embark on a concerted effort to address issues of justice, of class. To be honest, I expect this will be our most difficult work as Unitarian Universalists, the work we want to avoid." I know that holds true for me.

Here are but a couple of disturbing truths, stirred by Mary Elizabeth Hobgood's incisive chapter "An Ethical Agenda for Elites" in her book *Dismantling Privilege: An Ethics of Accountability*. First, although I often self-identify as "middle-class," our family income, certainly prior to semi-retirement, compared to most American wage earners, is anything but middle.

Second, my family, like that of so many other Unitarian Universalists, continues to unconsciously derive unearned benefits and advantages from the lower tier of the working class. As Hobgood puts it: "You and I are supported by whole armies of subordinate groups in so-called private homes and workplaces. These subordinates usually make and clean the clothes of the dominant groups; pick, package, and cook our food; clean up our messes; take care of our children, service our cars, planes, appliances, hospitals, and schools; and collect and process our garbage."

A Unitarian Universalist colleague recounts a routine of the comic Chris Rock that's relevant to the issue of economic privilege. Rock talks about how angry white men are whining these days that they're losing everything. "We're losing everything! We're losing everything!" "Like what?" Rock asks. He goes on, "Not even the white usher in this theatre would change places with me—and *I'm rich*. That's how good it is to be white!"

The WHAMMM constituency unquestionably holds the lion's share of public power in this land. As men's activist Paul Kivel puts it: "If as a man, you don't notice the culture of power, it's because you're inside it!" Our very language favors men with such proverbial phrases as power plays, power brokers, power lunches, power tools, power trips.

Nonetheless, to be sure, men pay a price for our privilege and power. Being on top costs. Steve Smith rightly notes, "On average in the United States, men are less successful than women in meeting our fundamental needs of life, health, safety, shelter, and love. . . . Men are powerful yet lonely, vulnerable, sick, homeless and dead."

Yet male power remains real, despite the genuine misery it dumps on the doorsteps of men. The bottom line: most children, youth, and female adults recognize that men receive more privileges and entitlements than they do.

Anthony Astrachan asserts that men have conventionally brandished four kinds of power: (1) the power to name; (2) the power to mobilize destructive aggression; (3) the power to organize societal, economic, and political life; and (4) the power to direct others' uses of skills. And, furthermore, these forms of power are traditionally handed down to men by society or learned from their fathers, and the temptation is to use them to overpower women and other men.

I recently saw a full-page power ad in a mainline magazine that pictured a sexy woman in a bathing suit next to a bottle of Chivas Regal whisky with two simple phrases bridging the body and the bottle: "Yes, God is a man. When you know . . . Chivas Regal." The implications are obvious: men are in the know, men hold the power, men can get any women they desire, and men are even identifiable with God itself! A fantasy of full-blown omnipotence, if you will.

Power in American culture, as defined by the men who conventionally wield it, is essentially reducible to dominance: power *over*. This "might makes right" attitude is evidenced in the war our American government initiated against Iraq. Machismo braided with arrogance, greed, and vengeance is a deadly combination.

Such hypermasculinity invariably creates a toxic mindset that devalues difference and, moreover, equates weakness with femininity, often with gayness. In this warped scenario "real" men can't afford to appear unsure, conciliatory, or afraid, lest they be ridiculed as sissies. Consequently, such males grow hell-bent on overpowering, to the point of wanton destruction, any person or land that poses a threat to their shaky egos. The irony is that such male bullies are profoundly insecure, operating from fear—their inner coward.

In *The Elder Within: The Source of Mature Masculinity*, Terry Jones rightly concludes that a degraded masculinity produces "the man who abuses his children, the politician who takes advantage of his constituency, the minister who hates homosexuals, the gang-banger who inflicts pain, the absent father and the tyrant boss . . . who all have one thing in common. They're all boys-in-men's bodies."

To worsen matters, the world mistakes these emotionally stunted and morally wayward boys for mature men and all too frequently rewards them with the power to run our very governments.

Yet Men Feel Powerless

Even so, despite the definite power base of males in contemporary life, there exist ample illustrations of men who exude powerlessness in their daily journeys. Let me share but two examples: one from the world of a WHAMMMer, the other from a non-WHAMMMer perspective.

The first story, from Pat Conroy's novel *The Prince of Tides*, portrays the mushrooming predicament of many WHAMMMers. The lead character, Tom Wingo, is a former high-school quarterback who has grown up in South Carolina, well schooled in the patterns of racism. He's considered "wicked and wrong," by progressive culture, and due to a change of heart, he gets involved in civil rights.

Then Wingo becomes involved in an exclusively male ROTC program and is vilified by those offended by the uniform. He changes for a second time and partakes in anti-military demonstrations. Just when he feels that he's evolved to higher moral ground, the women's liberation movement "bushwhacks" him, and he finds himself on the wrong side of the "barricades" yet again. Wingo laments, "This hasn't been an easy century to endure. . . . I seem to embody everything that's wrong with the twentieth century. . . ." In essence, Wingo feels downright powerless.

The second story of powerlessness arrives from a different place and perspective. It depicts the quiet yet insistent dignity of African-American agitators wrangling with the debilitating, life-long effects of racism.

The comedian-activist Dick Gregory tells the story of how, in an auditorium in Jackson, Mississippi several decades ago, he heard an older black man give a speech about how he'd been involved in a voter registration campaign and had been jailed for killing someone sent to burn his house in reprisal.

This man said: "I didn't mind going to jail for freedom, no, I wouldn't even mind being killed for freedom. But my wife and I were married for a long time, and well, you know I ain't ever spent a night away from home. And while I was in jail, my wife died." And he broke down weeping.

Gregory recalls how he felt listening to his elder:

> His story destroyed me. This man, my brave brother, bucked and rose up and fought the system for me, and he went to jail for me, and he lost his wife for me. He had gone out on the battle lines and demonstrated for a tomorrow he wouldn't ever see, for jobs and rights he might not even be qualified to benefit from. An elderly man from a country town who never spent a night away from his wife in his married life. And he went to jail for me and being away killed her.

Here are but two stories of persons who embody the same gender yet different races, both seeking freedom from perceived or actual oppression. As we can see, disempowerment of any kind, whatever its origin, diminishes self and others. Whereas imperious power corrupts, persistent powerlessness corrupts absolutely.

Claiming Our Power from Within

So, how do men escape this destructive power/powerlessness bind? Well, some never do. And pundits occasionally suggest that men should abandon power altogether and start over from scratch. But this seems a foolish, even cruel, suggestion, especially for men struggling on the margins of existence—burdened by oppressive, unfair treatment. If anything, genuinely disempowered males need to be able to both receive and create fresh fonts of real clout and sway.

And what about those men (predominantly the WHAMMMers) who are situated in seats of ostensible power? Well, for starters, we'd be sage to relinquish, then redistribute, some of our might in pursuit of greater justice for all, in addition to risking new sources of strength within our own souls. I offer two illustrations of men who've done just that: one displaying moral bravery in the political arena; the other incarnating a spiritual breakthrough in his family—both accessing afresh their inner power.

The first story signals an example of high moral courage displayed by George Ryan, a conservative Republican governor of Illinois. During the final days of his office, Ryan recently emptied Death Row in a sweeping order that spared 167 convicted murderers: 163 men and 4 women, who've served a collective 2,000 years for the murders of more than 250 people.

Condemning the capital punishment system as fundamentally flawed, Governor Ryan commuted all Illinois death sentences to prison terms of life or less, the largest such emptying of Death Row in history. His move was seen by many as the most significant statement questioning capital punishment since the Supreme Court struck down all state death penalty laws in 1972. Ryan's judgment unflinchingly challenged other states to engage in serious review of their own inadequate processes of justice.

What makes this deed all the more noteworthy is that Ryan's gubernatorial tenure generally had been marked by moral mediocrity. Furthermore, now, even as his legacy has been secured as a leading critic of state-sponsored execution, Ryan faces possible indictment in a previous corruption scandal that stopped him from seeking re-election.

Like most political leaders in places of privileged decision-making, George Ryan has had a checkered career, but on this particular issue he showed gutsy, principled behavior. Ryan blended high ethics with high power. Using the immense clout granted him as Governor, Ryan chose to use it constructively and compassionately. To be sure, he possessed sizable *external* power, but he claimed, then employed, it from an *internal* source.

As Ryan put it, "The legislature couldn't reform the capital punishment system. Lawmakers won't repeal it. But I won't stand for it." Wherever you stand on the institution of the death penalty, few of us would question that our country needs bold leadership in reforming the criminal justice system. And, moreover, I think you'd agree that George Ryan displayed mature masculinity in wielding his power in what he deemed a responsible way: researching the issues diligently, listening to all sides reasonably, probing his conscience relentlessly.

This was an inordinately difficult and unpopular decision to render. While a progressive minority in this land will commend Ryan, his verdict will draw scorn from the bulk of Americans. Even his wife Lura Lynn was angry and disappointed at her husband's decision. But as Ryan ultimately framed it on January 11, 2003, "Even if the exercise of my power becomes my burden, I'll bear it, because our Constitution compels it. I've lost a lot of sleep along the way, but tonight I'm going to sleep well, knowing in my heart I made the right decision."

While being governor granted Ryan the power to effect this decision, it was truly born of inner spiritual wellsprings. Ryan's office didn't deliver this verdict; his conscience did. Ryan's example should impel men everywhere, whatever privilege we possess or station we occupy, to claim our true strength from deep within, venturing daily decisions that marry ethics and power.

My second example is familial, not political. It shows how one economically secure, outwardly successful man, a partial WHAMMMer if you will, made a courageous move to garner some enduring integrity in his personal life. A leader in our San Diego Men's Fellowship, Eduardo accomplished in the private realm what Ryan performed in the public. Both were activated by conscience power, emboldened from within.

Here's Eduardo's personal testimony of empowerment.

> My concept of personal power used to focus on professional and financial success. It took a painful breakup in a relationship to allow me to see how disjointed my true inner power was from outward appearances of success.

86

The really difficult issues—reconciling my spiritual beliefs with my sexual life, learning how to interact in a healthy way with family members, interacting with other men without fear—were daunting. It took courage to venture into a group of men willing to speak openly about these issues. It was the best step I ever took.

I learned that I wasn't alone. I could share my hopes and fears with other men. Slowly, with support and encouragement from my newfound brothers, I began the journey into the inner reaches of myself that I had avoided for so long. The journey isn't over, but I'm grateful for the company of other courageous men to share the ride.

Like my chosen faith, our San Diego Unitarian Universalist Men's Fellowship calls me to be a more alive and whole person. The power of sharing at a personal and often intimate level with other men reaches me in a way that other forms of spiritual practice simply don't. Our Men's Fellowship is, for me, our Unitarian Universalist religion put into practice at a very personal level.

My soul-deep struggle has been how to live a healthy personal life as a gay man. For years, my Mexican Catholic upbringing led me to deny my sexuality or to express it in ultimately unfulfilling ways. Coming into a circle of caring, respectful men has inspired me to begin, and continue, the process of integrating my sexual being with a spiritually fulfilling personal life. It has changed my life.

Eduardo has dared to access much-needed healing and vitalizing strength that come not from the economy or politics or societal endorsement but from deep, deep within. From a spiritual place.

In actuality, whether men are powerful or powerless, we often expend too much effort scrambling for temporary forms of strength or control from transient sources. Mature liberal religious masculinity impels men to claim power from a spiritual locus rather than heredity, materiality, or status. It arrives from an interior source—whether one calls it an inner or higher power.

Diversifying Our Power Usage

It's my measured experience that power is like love—the more it expands, the larger everyone's portion grows. Once we ground our primary power source in the innermost realm, as did George and Eduardo, then we're progressively freed to diversify our means of wielding power. And, in so doing, we move ourselves closer toward mature liberal religious masculinity.

One caveat. Clearly, my chosen categories of exerting power possess cross-gender applications. But remember, I'm a man addressing issues of men in this book. I'm laboring on my own gender's homework assignments and challenges—not those of women. Naturally, women are welcome, nay, encouraged, to pluck lessons for their own sojourns.

Leaders: Power AHEAD

No matter how immobilized our situation may appear, you and I possess the capacity to advance. Unless we're comatose, we can alter our lives, even if gradually, inch by inch. Visionary men are those who dare to keep moving forward, especially when fellow travelers tend to lose their bearings.

It's my measured opinion that there exists a dearth of empowered and empowering male leaders in our Unitarian Universalist culture today, both in our seminaries and congregations. We're losing men to ministry, in part, because those guys who hanker to be potentates realize that's no longer a viable option in a movement that aspires to be more inclusive and egalitarian.

But I sense an additional explanation. Men who have yet to discover, let alone unleash, their inner might or who are prone to bouts of spinelessness are deterred as well, for ministry requires immense spiritual fortitude. Given the gender power shifts and confusions in contemporary culture, one can no longer assume that adult men are natural leaders. Many are outright passive and reactive, spongy and weak.

The current numbers of males in our Unitarian Universalist seminaries range roughly from 15% to 30%. I believe those figures will grow if men are encouraged to claim, then embody, their profoundest desires and voices of authority. Probably the best way to lure stronger males into ministry is by cultivating healthy empowerment in our young boys. We must groom youngsters to become emotionally resilient and morally resolute. We need to assist in the formation of boys into men, finally into brothers.

Our culture is clamoring for male figures willing to step out, move forward, and power ahead—simply to lead. Authority is related to the word *augment*, the capacity to make something grow, increase, and expand. But if men are shrinking, it's hard to make something else swell. To be an authority means to author from our deepest and dearest down places. Men must reconnect with our passional drives, so we'll become dependable authority figures rather than volatile authoritarian ones.

Henry Ford put it bluntly: "The question, who ought to be boss, is like asking, 'Who ought to be the tenor in the quartet?' Obviously, the person who can sing tenor!" The empowering man willingly strides ahead and fulfills a leadership task, flourishing in the role, neither shunning nor abusing it.

Law professor and activist Derrick Bell has stood tall for his principles on various occasions, even at the price of being fired from Harvard University. Bell, in supporting women and minorities in his unswerving commitment to inclusion, consistently leads from an internally based authority, born of a highly sensitized conscience. In his latest book, *Ethical Ambition*, Bell avers that one can be both ambitious and ethical while sparring for full-force equality.

A traditional West African song captures the proper moral balance in the pursuit of being a leader with character:

> Do not seek too much fame,
> but do not seek obscurity.
> Be proud.
> But do not remind the world of your deeds.
> Excel when you must,
> but do not excel the world.

Many heroes are not yet born.
Many have already died,
To be alive to hear this song is a victory.

James Hillman, in his book *Kinds of Power: A Guide to Its Intelligent Uses*, relates that John Adams, our second American president and erstwhile Unitarian, a capable though somewhat modest and stubborn man, admitted to a "passion for distinction." Healthy male leaders know our unique gifts without gloating about them. They pursue honor and achieve stature without subverting others. They exemplify a "passion for distinction," yet know when to step offstage and operate in the background.

Delegators: Power TO

Alas, men are prone to hoard might, once we garner some. Indeed, in the social realm, power often has to be wrested from WHAMMMers. Frederick Douglass minced no words in the 19th century when addressing racial inequities:

> This struggle may be a moral one or it may be both moral and physical; but it must be a struggle. Power concedes nothing without a demand; it never did and it never will. Find out what people will submit to, and you have found out the exact amount of injustice which will be imposed upon them. The limits of tyrants are prescribed by the endurance of those whom they oppress.

Douglass goes right to the heart of what it means to be the oppressed and the oppressor, and how hardened are the chains that imprison both. The relevance of his words obtains today.

Tyrants aren't the only ones compelled by an insatiable need to be in charge. I understand the craving. I count myself among those men who are driven by an excessive urge to control my self, my environment, and, consequently, often the moves of those around me, especially my dearest companions. It's partially an attempt to keep from being "out of control." But while such control may give me momentary security, it can drive others crazy. In truth, it's a disguised form of power *over* others.

Being a control freak doesn't empower anyone; it invariably disempowers. The strange key to staying empowered as a delegator is that we retain agency—for in useful relinquishment, we give a task away to another or we step aside so that someone else, who's been waiting in the wings, might rise to the forefront. We say, in effect: "It's your turn now. You have the capacity to assume the helm. I charge and bless you, my brother/my sister, with this hallowed task."

Delegation is a religious act, for it pushes us off our high horse. It divests us of power we never "owned" anyway. Furthermore, delegating is a humbling reminder that while we may be irreplaceable, we aren't indispensable—no one is.

Delegation means that we realize our importance without succumbing to hubris. There are other qualified people who can handle a job as adroitly as we can, sometimes more so. If we are members of WHAMMM, we've been the undeserved beneficiaries of the longest affirmative action program in history; now it's our season to move back, turn over control, and surrender some power.

But, oh, that's hard. Can you empathize with how agonizingly difficult, yet how crucial, it is for men who bask in power or cling to it even beyond the grave (through wills and the like) finally to delegate power, to pass it on?

Here's a painful yet instructive example. A couple decades ago, radical feminist theologian Mary Daly was speaking at our General Assembly on her book *Beyond God the Father*, which was back then and still is a revolutionary volume. After an unsettling address that was particularly hard for men to swallow, up popped a slew of male hands, desperate to state the first questions and, moreover, to set the record straight by rebutting this outspoken feminist. But Mary Daly held the mike and made the initial move by firmly setting boundaries: "The first several questions will be offered by those who seldom get the first word during public discourse, let alone possess the guts to speak out loud . . . namely, the women in the room. We may get to you guys later on, if there's time."

As the controlling presence in the room, Daly was delegating power to women, actually reallocating it in a fresh, albeit disconcerting, fashion, especially for card-carriers of "the old boys' club." That evening signaled men stepping aside so that women could step ahead—another version of affirmative action, or getting power into the hands of those with less of it.

Another illustration. In our final year of lengthy ministry in San Diego, one of my closing chores as a co-minister was to cease clinging tightly to "my church." It was time to pass on tasks, to let go of results, to remind myself and others that this particular male leader was leaving and that they were staying. It was amazing how many things I had been controlling, lots without my even realizing it. I bet Carolyn, my partner in life and ministry, would echo my sentiments.

As Andre Gide declared, "Great art is never completed, only surrendered." The same holds true with ministerial matches; they're never finished, only surrendered into the next set of hands.

Frankly, I see delegation as a sacred warm-up for the time when we relinquish whatever power we still possess at the time of death. It's necessary practice for ultimately releasing all our life-outcomes into the grasp of the creative unknown, mystery, divine companionship, if you will.

Caregivers: Power FOR

Related to the art of delegating power is learning how to function appropriately as a caregiver. The song "He Ain't Heavy, He's My Brother" comes to mind. For, in every brothering adventure, there are times when we're charged to carry another person, not just a child but an adult, not just a woman but a man, not just physically but emotionally, maybe financially or spiritually as well.

Men in history have known how to protect other men, even provide for them, but directly transporting or nursing them—being a caring brother up-close and personal—is unexplored territory for most of us. Indeed, to carry or be carried is viewed more as a badge of weakness than of strength in our macho world.

This caregiving dimension of male empowerment can only be appreciated if we've already endorsed the underlying assumptions of *Save the Males*. First, I'm a man by birth, but I become a brother by choice. Second, all men are my brothers. Third, this bedrock brothering attitude mandates me to relate respectfully to myself, other men, women, children, and all living entities.

Once we've understood the full-fledged charge and responsibility of brothering, we're able to carry one another, out of deep duty married to deep joy. I think of the men in our UU Men's Fellowship who've energetically practiced the power of caregiving with respect to other men.

One man has made regular telephone calls to men in the fellowship inquiring, in Quaker fashion, about their well-being: "How goes it with thy spirit?" He doesn't phone to make a request or garner a recruit. Antonio calls because he cares. Another guy, Eldrick, has taken as his sole Sunday mission, after worship, to greet men he's never seen before in church. A third man, Dean, has been making occasional house calls, in particular to men who are physically sick, socially isolated, or emotionally distraught.

Another man, along with his partner and another couple, essentially overhauled the existence of one of our senior men, Jack, who had been living pretty much as a recluse and was quickly going downhill. This caregiving crew cleaned out his messy home, revitalized Jack's spirit, transported him hither and yon, and even accompanied him to an out-of-state college reunion. They kept caring in critical ways until the day he died. Jack had never been so lovingly cared for, or carried, in the previous seven decades of his life as he was by this male-inspired brigade. Resultingly, this lonely elder donated a $100,000 gift to our church specifically earmarked for a caregiving program. Jack wanted the gift of caring to be extended to others like himself.

Of course, the key is to walk the fine line between caregiving and caretaking, between lifting another brother when he needs it and lugging him when *we* need it.

There have been times in my own brothering encounters when it would have been better if I'd shed the ministerial role and simply related man-to-man. If power comes with your job, as with mine, boundaries must be crystal-clear, not leaky. Furthermore, adult males must be vigilant never to transgress the power differential between ourselves and boys or teenage youth.

Yet we can't summarily abandon the caregiving mode of power because of its potential misuse. Genuinely caring brothers choose to touch all whom they engage in appropriate ways, physically and emotionally. A church's job is to create safe havens for everyone's spiritual growth, from cradle to grave.

Christian philosopher Beatrice Bruteau reminds us that the greatest revolution in human history occurred on Maundy Thursday, when Jesus washed the feet of his disciples. Until that moment the basic human mission had been for someone, invariably a man, to get ahead—climbing over and contending against rather than caringly treating another person as your equal.

Collaborators: Power ALONGSIDE

> Don't walk in front of me—I may not follow. Don't walk behind me—I may not lead. Walk beside me and just be my friend.
>
> —Albert Camus

Men of true strength willingly share power as delegators, as care-givers, and as collaborators. Consider the resources of a jazz combo as a harmonious, creative alliance of soloists. A thoughtful teammate is neither jealous nor frightened to divide burdens and multiply the glory.

I reflect upon Senator Paul Wellstone, the Democrat from Minnesota who was killed the fall of 2002 in a tragic plane crash. Wellstone was the only vulnerable incumbent to vote against the resolution that would give President Bush war powers. He bravely told the Senate: "Acting now on our own might be a sign of our power, but acting sensibly and in a measured way in concert with our allies . . . would be a sign of our strength."

Wellstone was pinpointing the crucial difference between unilateral and relational power, a distinction that power-hoarders habitually choose to ignore.

Even as I'm writing this book, our current American administration has continued to advance our sovereign right to make war alone—a thrust that, from my vantage point, is both political poppycock and moral wrong-headedness. Other international powers such as France, Germany and Russia have vigorously tried to put their feet down in favor of tough and thorough cooperative inspections, but to no avail.

The problems of weapons of mass destruction as well as world terrorism are stubborn and difficult realities that demand not independent but collaborative power wielding. Male leaders must learn how to work jointly when it comes to peacemaking and justice-building. The art of relational power is desperately required in our interpersonal as well as international crises. Let us saunter neither ahead nor behind, but alongside other human beings. Let us move in the world as respectful allies.

John Stoltenberg puts it baldly: "The core of one's being must love justice more than manhood! Justice building is acting not in one's self-interest but acting in the interest of one's own best self!" Such a ringing mandate regularly requires power-sharing, working as colleagues—literally "leagued together" in pursuit of a common purpose.

Let me close this segment with a poignant story, told by Rabbi David Wolpe in *Teaching Your Children About God*, that is surely germane to our brothering quests, whether familial or worldwide.

A boy and his father were walking along a road when they came across a large stone. The boy said to his father, "Do you think if I use all my strength, I can move this rock?" His father answered, "If you use all your strength, I'm sure you can do it." The boy began to push the rock. Exerting himself as much as he could, he pushed and pushed. The rock didn't move. Discouraged, he said to his father, "You were wrong. I can't do it." His father placed his arm around the boy's shoulder and said, "No, son. You didn't use all your strength—you didn't ask *me* to help."

Brothers call in others, whether laboring locally or globally.

Resisters and Reconcilers: Power AGAINST and ACROSS

> Holding each other close across differences, beyond conflict, through change, is an act of resistance.
>
> —bell hooks

95

We Unitarian Universalists are very good at calling the evil
to account. We must never stop doing that. But what we
need to understand as well is that sometimes in the heat
of the whirlwind, in the midst of the burning bush, the
truly radical, truly courageous position is that of the medi-
ator, the intercessor, the healer, and the lover.

—Bill Schulz

Men must be versatile enough to negotiate what I call the R-and-R
plan: *resistance*, or powering *against* a wrong, and *reconciliation*, or powering
across chasms toward a mutually satisfying result. In mature liberal religious masculinity, resistance and reconciliation function as yin-yang allies.

A few words about each.

First, *resistance*. There exists a live, contentious struggle between
theocracy and democracy in our free land. The radical religious right is
gaining political power in America and poses a real threat to our consti-
tutional freedoms, where only those people with the "proper" religious
viewpoint will be considered first-class citizens.

This state of affairs is hardly news to Unitarian Universalists, yet it's
easy to be lulled into an inactivity that disempowers us, rather than staying awake, which would empower us.

Therefore, progressive religious men who are ardent supporters of
religious liberty and pluralism must make concerted efforts to reclaim
American history, register and mobilize voters, and, most importantly, create inclusive and diverse brothering communities where we worship.
Liberative men must also resist demonizing, hate-crimes, and dogmatism
and intolerance wherever they rear their ugly heads. As Unitarian
Universalist professor Sharon Welch witnesses: "To stop resisting, even
when success is unimaginable, is to die."

Liberal men can too readily succumb to wishy-washiness. Poet
Robert Frost tenders a biting critique of religious liberals that we've simply got to outgrow: "A liberal is one often too broadminded to even take
his or her own side in a quarrel." On the contrary, responsible liberal men

show spine, take stands, and resist vehemently. As Coretta Scott King says, "it's vitally important that we endorse zero tolerance for bigotry."

Assuming the mantle of shameless defiance not only makes a difference in society but emboldens the resisters as nothing else can. Men who are persistent protesters of injustice are indisputably among the most vital guys you'll ever meet.

The companion virtue to resistance is *reconciliation*. Grown-up liberal religious men are committed to employing these empowering postures in tandem.

I belong to a small local band of peacemakers called the Fellowship of Reconciliation—an international, interfaith organization founded in 1914. I assume it was christened thus, not as the Fellowship of Peace, Justice, or Mercy, because the founders wanted to challenge us, and they did. Reconciliation is the most difficult of life's encounters, since it entails the coming together, with some measure of harmony, of individuals who have been sundered, sometimes grievously so. No tougher religious art or skill exists, assuredly for men, than the pursuit of reconciliation, be it between sparring partners or warring nations.

To illustrate my point, I reference a disturbing phrase nestled in the familiar, comforting 23rd Psalm that reminds us of the ever-present call to be reconcilers and reconciled: "Thou preparest a table before me in the presence of my enemies." Now, setting a table before family or friends hardly poses a religious challenge for men, unless, of course, we're at odds with our own kin. But being charged by Yahweh to share company with our foes—literally, to break bread with our enemies—constitutes the consummate demand of mighty love.

Reconciliation is the process of powering across gulfs toward workable connections and caring communion. It takes every ounce as much strength as being a leader, a delegator, a caregiver, a collaborator, and a resister.

Let me close this segment with a male-dominated story in which resistance and reconciliation are faithfully, even successfully, braided.

It's the ongoing story, in my hometown of San Diego, of the Tariq Khamisa Foundation—committed to breaking the escalating cycle of youth violence and planting seeds of hope for our children's future.

While delivering pizza on a cool San Diego night in January of 1995, a shot rang out and young Tariq Khamisa fell mortally wounded. At the other end of the gun was a 14-year-old gang member.

From the beginning, Azim Khamisa, the dead boy's father, saw "victims at both ends of the gun." And so he reached out, across culture and religion, to the shooter's family. Azim embraced the boy's grandfather, Ples Felix, and asked him to join forces against youth violence. Out of their remarkable union was born the Tariq Khamisa Foundation, whose sole purpose is to stop children from killing children.

TKF brings its message of peace and nonviolent choices to school-children through its innovative Violence Impact Forum program, a lively, multimedia presentation. The Forum has been presented to over 10,000 children in the fourth through ninth grades, with a resultant reduction in attitudes and behaviors that lead to gangs, revenge, and violence.

The senseless shooting of Tariq Khamisa has sparked the creation of a powerful violence prevention program that works. As Azim puts it:

> I will mourn Tariq's death for the rest of my life. Now, however, my grief has been transformed into a powerful commitment to change. Change is urgently needed in a society where children kill children.

The Tariq Khamisa Foundation constitutes a saving story launched by one brave man achingly in quest of healing power drawn from his inner being. It depicts an impressive recovery bridging three generations of men. While it's likely more dramatic than what you or I may encounter first-hand in our own journeys, we can still identify with its power at some visceral, soul-deep level. Why? Because there's already been, or will surely come, a time in our life-travels where we too must be united with our opposition, and the unifying cement requires our utmost respect and brave compromise amidst shared pain.

Perhaps it's an agonizing divorce, or a seemingly irretrievable break with a child, or a devastating loss at work—any wrenching situation where everyone involved slumps in inexpressible anguish.

So, during our lifetimes, we men and women undergo, in common, the realities of massive sorrow and inexplicable joy, and more than that,

we also share the gift of earth and the challenge of dying. All these expe-
riences should make us committed to doing our part to resist and to reconcile, to stop the cycle of violence, to affirm the full dignity of every
traveler we meet along the path.

Followers: Power UNDER

Following another person is frequently judged to be a disguised form
of subservience or powerlessness. This couldn't be farther from the truth.
Followers are servants, and, as such, they embody power in one of its
richest and most resourceful expressions.

Empowered and empowering men are versatile: leading, delegating,
caregiving, collaborating, resisting, reconciling, and, yes, following. A
modest phrase from the political philosopher John Locke has come to
assume considerable importance in my understanding of might. He said:
"Power is the ability to cause or receive change." Conventionally, men are
depicted as change-agents but seldom portrayed as pilgrims brave enough
to *receive* change. Yet, in point of fact, an evolved man is ambidextrous:
willing both to catalyze and to undergo change.

An unthreatened wielder of power is one who's able to reside under
the rule (not thumb) of others rather than always holding sway at the
mountaintop. The good leader can be a good follower. If you wish,
another word for follower is servant, not so much a suffering as a cheer-
ful one.

I always get a kick out of the quote attributed to politician Benjamin
Disraeli (1804–1881): "I must follow the people, for I am their leader!"
Isn't it startling, if not disturbing, to recognize that there have been thou-
sands of books written on leadership and none on the art of follower-
ship? I've heard plenty of college presidents tell their student bodies that
schools are meant to train leaders. I've yet to hear anyone profess to train
followers. But that just may be one of the most important, if toilsome,
imperatives for men.

Alas, too few of the dominant men in our modern world truly
know how to be humble and responsive followers. And yet authentic
empowerment is marked by rhythm: men knowing when to be out front,

when to take up the rear, and when to walk hand-in-hand. It's precisely this kind of flexibility that will pry men loose from the power/power-lessness vise.

There's a delightful story of Ralph Waldo Emerson as a child. He was watching a lumberjack sawing up some wood. The task was beyond young Waldo's strength, but finally he perceived a way to be useful. "May I," Emerson asked, "do some grunting for you?" Well, empowering men are never loath to do grunt work, to play minor roles or perform menial chores, to assist in the background.

Two more examples of empowering male servants, one from literature, the other from real life.

In Herman Hesse's story "Journey to the East" we behold a band of people on a mythical journey, probably representing Hesse's own spiritual quest. The central figure of this story is Leo, who accompanies the party as the servant who does their scut-work, but who also imbues them with his spirit and song. He's a person of extraordinary presence. All goes well until Leo disappears. Then the group falls into disarray, and the journey is abandoned. They can't make it without the servant Leo.

The narrator, one of the party, after some years of wandering, finds Leo and is taken into the religious order that had sponsored the journey. There he discovers that Leo, whom he had known first as servant, was in fact the titular head of the order, its guiding spirit, and a great and noble leader. A classic example of a male who proves to be an empowering leader-servant.

And remember the words of one of our 20th-century moral guides, Dr. Martin Luther King, Jr., from his final speech:

> If any of you are around when I have to meet my day, I don't want a long funeral. And if you get somebody to deliver the eulogy, tell them not to talk too long. Tell them not to mention that I have a Nobel Peace Prize. That isn't important. Tell them not to mention that I have 300 or 400 hundred other awards. That's not important.
>
> I'd like someone to mention that day that Martin Luther King, Jr. tried to give his life serving others. I'd like

for somebody to say that Martin Luther King, Jr. tried to love somebody.

I want you to be able to say that day that I did try to feed the hungry. I want you to be able to say that I did try in my life to clothe the naked. I want you to say on that day that I did try in my life to visit those who were in prison, and I want you to say that I tried to love and serve humanity.

Epilogue

This chapter on "men and might" has outlined manifold ways of men powering toward greater justice and joy for our gender and all whom we touch. A broad smorgasbord of power-options is desirable in an era when men are perceived to be ultra-strong yet often experience themselves as burdened or inadequate.

Our liberal religious church should be a refuge from the storm as well as a house of enlightenment or embrace, but, moreover, it must fundamentally become a place of empowerment. Yes, our progressive tribes demand stout-souled men who are willing to be ambidextrous and responsible wielders of power.

May we nurture brothering circles in our local congregations where a man (whether decorated with might or downtrodden with oppression or saddled with a blend of the two) can join our ranks and hear words similar to these:

Dear Brother,

May you be emboldened in our midst to open your heart to love, surrender your soul to anguish, expand your mind to wisdom, lift your spirit in aspiration, treat your body as a wondrous gift, nudge your conscience to change society . . . release your burdens and be freed.

For you are, indeed, a worthy man. You are capable. You are lovable. You are singular and precious. You are a powerful being. And, in our beloved community, we will comfort and challenge you to employ your full power in pursuit of the good, the true, and the beautiful.

For in our ranks you will be able to marry ethics and power.

Chapter 5: Saying Yes to Aggression and No to Violence

I'm a pragmatic hoper. In the final analysis, I agree with Stephen Boyd, who says,

> Men aren't inherently or irreversibly violent, relationally incompetent, emotionally constipated, and sexually compulsive. To the extent that we manifest these characteristics, we do so not because we are male, but because we've experienced violent socialization and conditioning processes that have required or produced this kind of behavior and we've chosen to accept, or adopt, these ways of being, thinking, and acting.

I contend that men can transform our histories of damaged and damaging masculinity. We can—indeed we must—become more mature liberal religious brothers. Changing men will change our world.

One of the thorny yet useful distinctions for contemporary men to negotiate lies at the heart of this chapter: namely, saying yes to *aggression*, or soul-force, and saying no to *violence*, or unwarranted destruction.

Our Demonic Male Legacy

> There is no such thing as paradise, not in the South Seas, not in southern Greece, not anywhere. There never has been. To find a better world we must look not to a romanticized and dishonest dream forever receding into the

primitive past, but to a future that rests on a proper understanding of ourselves.

—Dale Peterson and Richard Wrangham

Before men can make substantial progress toward evolving a more responsible and responsive masculinity, we've got to deal with our biologically rooted inheritance, in addition to the "violent socialization" that Boyd referenced.

In *Demonic Males: Apes and the Origins of Human Violence*, Dale Peterson and Richard Wrangham claim that hyperviolent social behavior is deeply rooted in male human genes and common among our closest primate relatives. Rapes, beatings, and killings are as common among the great apes as they are among us. After 40 years of gorilla- and chimpanzee-watching, these authors find it hard not to conclude that human males are evolutionary heirs of male ape aggression.

Although history's evidence is overwhelming and depressing, these tandem authors are not die-hard biological determinists. They offer a modicum of hope: "With an evolutionary perspective we can firmly reject the pessimists who say it has to stay that way. Male demonism is not inevitable." The authors refer to bigger brains and the development of language, moral codes, a justice system, and democratic governments as countervalents to our in-bred violence.

Their thesis is congruent with our life-affirming Unitarian Universalist gospel that's grounded in observable reality. Liberal religion claims that men are capable of migrating from our checkered, oft-disgraceful, fate toward a nobler destiny, one that exudes gentle strength and kindly aggression. We can be compassionate beasts. As we progressively mature from boyhood to manhood, then on to brotherhood, we will be advancing from behavioral ruin toward soulful non-violence.

Two Intertwining Truths

Violence is an exquisitely complex phenomenon, with countless subtle variations; many of which are easy for humans to adroitly ignore, including principled Unitarian Universalist men. I offer two intertwining psycho-social truths, supplementing those of evolutionary biology, that corroborate that we humanoids are indeed violent creatures.

Violence is Pervasive

Human beings demonstrate an astounding array of violent attitudes and behaviors, both local and global, and all rooted in *violations of personhood*. Here's the way liberation theologian Robert McAfee Brown draws the linkage:

> Whatever violates another, in the sense of infringing upon or disregarding or abusing or denying that other, whether physical harm is involved or not, can be understood as an act of violence. The basic overall definition of violence would then become violation of personhood. When we talk about a "person" we are not talking about an object but about a subject. We are describing someone who is not quantifiable or interchangeable with another. Each person has unique worth.

This expansive definition is certainly in alignment with Unitarian Universalist values. Furthermore, when violence is defined this way, it's well nigh impossible for men to peg it as something occurring outside our own lives.

Just take a hard look at reality. Violations of personhood are perpetrated by and against men daily. Such violence happens via hostile remarks and dismissive attitudes. It occurs when fathers stand aloof from or overpower our children. It transpires whenever we consciously or inadvertently sabotage our partners or deride our colleagues, tune out youth or warehouse seniors. We miss the insidious scope of violence if we solely equate it with physical abuse, sexual misbehavior, warring destruction, or racial fury.

Violence is omnipresent in our culture. There is the violence of those who act out their frustrations. There is the violence of the respectable and powerful. There are acts of violence as well as states of violence. There is overt and covert, personal and institutional violence. Additionally, all social inequities perpetuate one another because each teaches us that it's okay for some people to dominate others. And the varieties of violence are interwoven. Violence against women and children will not be stopped unless violence against people of color, gays, lesbians, ethnic groups, disabled people, working-class folks, elders, and the rest is also eliminated.

We men—particularly good, sweet, caring guys like myself—desperately want to rid ourselves of the virulent virus of violence, but we can't. Some residue of violence lodges in our systems, personally and socially, all our days. However, while we're unable to stop violence, every man can curtail his attitudes and acts of violence, day by day, deed by deed.

Violence Begets Violence

Wounded in our upbringing, men wound in return. Violence becomes a self-enabling cycle. The German psychologist Alexander Mitscherlich has written that "society has torn the soul of the male, and into this tear demons have fled—demons of insecurity, selfishness, and despair." Remember that I'm explaining, not excusing, male attitudes and behaviors of violence.

However, men are not impotent to do something about our backgrounds. First, we can address, if not undo, some damage from our pasts through in-depth therapy and men's support groups. Second, we can vow to break, as much as possible, the vicious cycle of wrongs done unto us. Third, we can applaud the blessings we received from our upbringings and promise to pass similar gifts on to our own children.

I'm urging men to learn from our pasts, neither to bask nor to wallow in them. Too many of us remain stuck in the dysfunctionality of our boyhoods. We continue to live as developmentally arrested and rage-driven little guys, too scared and shaky to risk maturing into manhood, let alone brotherhood.

106

As adult men we've got to start demonstrating moral and spiritual guts in order to halt the rampaging cycle of violence in America—in its streets, its media, and its sports. The crimes committed in the name of our gender are astounding. As an adult man, I must do my fair share to diminish the swelling violence. We select it; we can reject it.

An example. I was reading a reputable sports magazine recently. I love sports both as a participant and as a spectator, but I'm appalled at the burgeoning level of male violence on and off the field, principally in hockey and football. Blatant, built-in brawling. Athletic contest is rarely about sportsmanship, even competition, any more; it's increasingly about trying to harm your opponent.

But the following anecdote crossed a new line. Sportswriter Rick Reilly was bemoaning that his teenage son was watching an enormously popular violent video game where acts of NFL football violence, with its attendant taunting and celebratory dances, are shown with realistic graphics.

Of course, there are tons of violent video games viewed by kids daily, but listen to this convoluted trail of immorality. Reilly writes, "The NFL fines players for these violent hits, then cashes in on the very same thing with licensed video games" that, in turn, enthrall our young. Violence begets violence. Indeed, in this case, it's unconscionably passed on from adult males to younger ones, with implicit blessing and mercenary intent. Shameful!

I challenge all men with this fundamental question: who will rise up and stop this societal destruction? Who among our male species is brave enough, assertive enough—make that aggressive enough—to blow the whistle on the escalating, gratuitous violence that's sanctioning vicious attitudes and behavior among our male offspring?

The Necessary Gift of Kindly Aggression

> God did not give us a spirit of timidity, but a spirit of power and love and self-control.
>
> —II Timothy 1:7

The virtues of zeal, fortitude, and perseverance are mean-
ingless without consideration of the aggressive compo-
nent that gives them vitality.

—William Meissner

I propose that one of the keys to breaking, or at least abating, this
pattern of unchecked, pan-generational violence is for men to learn and
practice ways of kindly aggression. This came home to me with cascad-
ing relevance when Unitarian Universalist colleague and friend Thandeka
referred me to a most perceptive volume by Kathleen J. Greider entitled
Reckoning with Aggression: Theology, Violence, and Vitality.

Greider's thesis untangles a saving message men need to heed at this
moment in history. She says that aggression, while ambiguous in our society, has usually been viewed as evil or sinful. If repaired, aggression can
be seen in its healthy light, neither as passivity nor hostility, and can incite
us to fight social ills and make the globe safer and more just. As she phrases it: "I am sure that few things in the world are more irresistible than gentle strength and strong gentleness. Perhaps aggression—reckoned with,
re-braided with love, and well cared for—will yield them both."

Greider navigates distinctions necessary to producing men sufficiently motivated to change the world. She claims that "*aggression* is significant energy, vigor, agency, enterprise, boldness and resilience; whereas
violence is force against persons, objects, or principles that intentionally or
unintentionally injures, damages, or destroys."

What will enable men to transform our internal, interpersonal, and
international strife is precisely an abundant supply of such vital, aggressive energy. Violence spawns violence; it's a futile route strewn with devastation. But quiescence and apathy are damaging as well. Hence, mature
males need to pursue the third way of passionate, forceful nonviolence.
In the words of Meir Berliner, who died fighting the Nazi SS at Treblinka:
"When oppressors give me two choices, I always take the third!"

Greider goes on to raise the kinds of questions that adult males need
to confront in embodying a mature liberal religious masculinity:

Is it possible to find or create among us a power finely tuned enough to destroy what needs to be destroyed—the structures of violence and other evils—without destroying each other?

Why is aggression generally characterized as undesirable and widely denied to subjugated classes, but its energies and powers often enjoyed and abused by dominant classes?

Recent studies reveal that not just an excess of testosterone but a deficiency can contribute to negative, violational behavior. I'll go one step further. While assertiveness training is important, it isn't a strong enough antidote to endemic injustice and suffering. Why? Because assertiveness usually begins and ends with personal catharsis, which seldom leads to substantive social change.

Men need to outgrow groveling niceness, faintheartedness of conscience, spongy backbones. We must develop, then practice, the arts of healthy, kindly aggression in order to expand the circle of maturation.

Aggression isn't an ugly word at root. It literally means taking action or moving forward: toward a person, a posture, a principle, or an event. It means eluding the grasp of lethargy or fright and advancing toward our goal. Men need to aggress what we value: to move *toward* someone in respect, to move *away* from lone-rangerism into nourishing solitude; to move *against* something in resistance. Of course, there will be subtle dangers to dodge. Our respect dare not breed docility. Our solitude can't slide into seclusion. Our resistance must avoid recklessness. But aggression is the ground-floor, animating energy that undergirds all brave, forward-moving deeds.

It starts with children and play. As Gestalt therapy addresses the theme:

> In order to make contact with the environment, in order to get needs met, the child must aggress into the environment. This is a healthy and necessary biological and psychological function. Life is not a passive matter. It is aggression that serves the life of the child; it allows distinctions to be made between the child and the larger world. Aggression, therefore, is essential for growth and learning.

I'm currently an assistant coach for our grandson Trevor's Little League team. It's all too tempting for adults (both coaches and parents) to overwhelm these youngsters, between 7 and 10 years of age, with our ostensible "wealth" of baseball savvy. It's usually preferable to transmit a few basic skills, affirm each kid constantly and personally, then shut our mouths and let them evolve in their own fashion.

Nonetheless, one of the universally appropriate pieces of advice for these little guys is to be "aggressive" rather than timid or passive at the plate when they bat. Whenever we ask the youngsters what single thing they most like to do in baseball, to a child, they say "hitting, hitting, hitting." So, we remind them that they will utterly miss out on that distinct pleasure unless they dare to use the piece of wood/aluminum resting in their hands to strike that swift-moving little spheroid!

Clearly, the most successful hitters in baseball, including Little League, are those who, when they see a decent pitch to hit, swing with resolve rather than freeze with fear. "Be aggressive, Trevor—when you see a pitch you like, drive it!"

Boys, followed by youth, then adult males, must progressively learn to express their aggression in constructive and vitalizing ways.

Robert Bly and other men's movement leaders have noted that the current crop of younger men are unduly mushy, weak-kneed, torpid. As he puts it:

> The soft or naive male in rejecting the obnoxious male traits has also abandoned the forceful and heroic aspects of masculinity, to the detriment of society. . . . [A] grown man six feet tall will allow another person to cross his boundaries, enter his psychic house, verbally abuse him, carry away his treasures and slam the door behind him; the invaded man will stand there with an ingratiating, confused smile on his face.

Mature men are appropriately aggressive. We set healthy boundaries and limits in every dimension of our lives. We learn how to express anger for impact rather than injury. Anger is truly among the toughest emotions for men to gainfully navigate. Our men's fellowship gatherings in San

Diego have been filled over the years with men who, like Robert, are consumed with "anger cemented with sadness and with shame at my own inadequacies." Here's an excerpt from one of Robert's potent poems that reveals his twisted, unresolved rage-filled tussle with his long-since dead father. It's entitled "questions I went to hell because of."

> How come you were never there how come
> you were drunk so much didn't you like me
> why did you and mommy fight all the time
> how come if you never hit me I still feel
> so bad how come I can't touch you how come
> you won't teach me how to be a man how
> come you're so mad all the time how come I
> feel so bad when I'm always trying my hardest how come
> I'm always
> afraid what can I do to
> make you like me.

In San Diego we've held various evening sessions as well as weekend renewals precisely on teaching one another how to be positively angry rather than either self-punishing, underhanded, compliant, explosive, or hostile: all destructive ways of venting naturally felt anger. We attempt to create a safe container for brothers like Robert to yell, dance, draw, pummel punching bags, play, and journal their rage through to constructive release.

The elders among us must assist in fortifying the conscience and vertebrae of this younger generation of brothers, by exemplifying the ways of kindly aggression . . . for we graybeards are often under-exercised in boldness as well. In truth, every brother resides somewhere on the pathway toward positive anger and kindly aggression. None of us has arrived at a conclusion point. Our job is to keep advancing in the right direction.

A fundamental way for men to launch the quest for healthy aggression is by locating what the Hindu *Upanishads* calls "our deep driving desires." Sadly, for the most part, men have suppressed our genuine appetites and ambitions, dutifully submitting to societally endorsed cravings for our gender—unquestionably, at grave cost to our inner lives. Lots

111

of men simply don't know who they are, where they're going, and what they're truly after.

Conversely, a healthy dose of aggression furnishes an enlivening curative to depression; for when we're aggressing, we press forth. Aggression restores passion to the masculine psyche and reinvigorates our rag-doll, listless beings.

It's a wholesome, wondrous sight watching men aggressively playing with children; aggressively combating injustice; aggressively doing household chores; aggressively carrying our brothers; aggressively setting firm, not flimsy, boundaries in an organization; aggressively abandoning addictions; aggressively competing in sports; aggressively mourning; aggressively meditating; aggressively fighting for result, not revenge. And, furthermore, you know what? Without aggression the intransigent problems of sexism and racism, economic injustice and homophobia will unlikely be touched, let alone dismantled.

Gandhi talked about committing "aggressive civil disobedience," and King chose to engage in "militant nonviolence." Justice-building and peace-making are never enterprises for the dispassionate of spirit or sluggish of body; they require joyful decisiveness and aggressive advocacy.

I know this to be true: without aggression, courage chickens out, love turns inept, generosity loses heart, and justice is schmaltzified.

One of our Unitarian Universalist brothers, Frank Withrow, recently spoke at his church's Super Bowl Sunday men's service. His talk "Who are the Real Men?" sparkles with the resolute energy of healthy aggression.

> In difficult times the refiner's fire often burns brightly and there are those who stand head and shoulders above others. There are those men whose physical stamina and strength bring out the best. They devote their lives to rescuing the endangered. They deserve the name heroes.
>
> But there are other real men who are not afraid to go against the tide of popular wisdom. They're not afraid to tell the king he has no clothes, the magician that his technology is hollow, the warrior that his fight is folly, and the lover that his love is self-indulgence. They're not afraid to

stand for high principles when all others bash those principles to bits on the hard rocks of patriotism. It's not hard
to join the U.S. Marines when all others are rushing to
join. It's often hard to stand against the winds of the time
and to speak out for peace and justice for all.

Mark Twain was not afraid to talk of the humanity of
all men including African Americans, doing this when the
wisdom of the land was the opposite of his beliefs.
Commander-in-chief Dwight David Eisenhower articulated well his position and warned us against the military
industrial complex.

Real men speak out for the things they believe.

Real men honor all living things.

Real men love others as themselves.

What the world needs now are a few real men!

Healthy Male Aggression

Despite our markedly diverse upbringings, every adult male can con-
jure up memories of friendly, firm, fair aggressive exchanges with another boy or teenager or man. We may more easily remember a batch of
negative encounters, but there are positive, encouraging incidents to
recall as well.

Here's one example, a light poem I wrote about the sacred tie with
my biological brother Phil entitled "Jousting Kin." It speaks of playful
aggressive scraps: in my case, openly wrestling with my brother, a slight-
ly older male whom I viewed with jumbled admiration and angst.
However, through it all, our brothering bond has remained a positive,
precious bond.

> Phil and Tom
> Brothers sparring affectionately
> From cradle forward
> Employing bodies, then words.

113

Healthy pugnacity
Tumbling outside on lush green
Arm-wrestling
Knee-football in the den
Vying for kingship on assorted hills
Stream of verbal tiffs
Happy pushes, jealous shoves
No harm, no foul
Laughter ripples
Roughhousing cements bond

Jousting with colleagues
Boundaries easily crossed
Jesting with mate
Gets touchy
Fencing with friends
Susceptible to wanton gashes
Own kids outgrow bedroom tussles

Visceral urge
Endures
One more scuffle
On old familiar turf
Then bury
Beloved Brothers
Side by side
In nearby vacant lot

Clearly, we males are starved for healthy rather than harmful touch. I tender another more gripping and potent illustration of how crucial it is to be "handled" in a safe, appropriate manner within our families of origin.

Here's Bert's testimony as tearfully revealed to his home congregation in San Diego.

> I was raised as the eldest in a family with two brothers and a sister. My full-time mother was intimately involved with her children. My father was distant and unavailable even

114

when he was home. I grew up believing my father really didn't like me very much.

At age 35, I had a profound experience. A therapist friend who used hypnosis in his practice offered to regress me back to my early childhood. I agreed mostly to see what it was like to be hypnotized.

During the experience I remembered a time when I was 18 months old. I was sitting on the wood floor of a line shack where my dad worked as a cryptographer for the railroad. We were together alone for the first time in my life; my mother was in the hospital giving birth to a little brother.

Dad was drinking. He was angry. He was crying as he spoke to the baby a few feet away sitting on the floor. He told the small child how awful his father had treated him when he was small. He sobbed about the horrible wounds he endured, and he spewed out rage that he felt toward a man he hadn't seen since he was a young boy. And then he made a promise. He promised the little boy that he would never touch him, lest he hurt him.

I couldn't get this powerful memory out of my head. It dominated my thoughts for weeks. I arranged to travel home for a visit, and I instantly confronted my father about my memory when I saw him.

He denied it all in the beginning, but then I recreated details about the room—the wooden chair with the black leather seat that squeaked when it turned, the sparse furnishings of the room, windows without glass or curtains, and the smell of dry desert air on that still night. I even recounted with verbatim accuracy what my father had said. He started to tremble and shake, then cry as I continued to recreate that memorable evening.

I told dad how powerful the memory had been for me, that it had changed my whole perception of our relationship. I now saw his distance as a way of protecting me.

I now believed he loved me greatly and his being unavailable was the only way he found to break a cycle of abuse that had been passed down from father to son.

My father and I hugged one another for the first time in our lives that night. I then enjoyed three years of closeness with my dad before he died. And when he died, I knew my father loved me.

Moreover, when I reconciled with my father, I also began to see men in a new way. I found myself wanting to be with men and talk with men about my changing perception of how we might be with one another. I wanted to touch and be touched by men in safe, caring ways.

I went to a men's group meeting at the First Unitarian Universalist Church of San Diego and discovered men there who wanted to be authentic, to share deeply in intimate circles of men. That was 18 years ago. My life has been changed forever.

Let me offer another concrete example of kindly male-to-male aggression.

One of the healthiest, non-invasive actions men can take is to massage one another's backs and hands. We've done back-massages in a train-line early on in men's gatherings, but hand-massaging poses a more radical venture and requires more time and trust. Yet whenever we've invited men to massage another man's hands in a caring dyad, not only is it relaxing and calming, but also it provides the first time most men have ever massaged another brother's hands. Hand-massage is a surprisingly audacious and important act of restorative *mano a mano* aggression.

Assertive men would likely contemplate a same-sex hand-massage; aggressive men undertake it. For handling another man is an aggressive deed; it moves us directly toward another man. It requires mutual consent. It requires chutzpah. It's nonviolent but aggressive.

After the hand-massage, we grant men time to talk about this physically intimate exchange, and abundant tears and heartfelt confessions consistently flow. Men's hands, softened by this simple exercise, are now strengthened to stroke others in soothing, not injurious ways.

Countless men have forthwith chosen to place in their wallets a pledge, crafted by UU Men's Fellowship member Tomas Firle, that charges us to employ our hands for embraces, caressing, creative activity and play, but never for damage.

The card reads:

> My Interpersonal No-Violence Pledge
> I SHALL NOT:
> —raise my voice or use threats to dominate others
> —raise my hands in an intimidating manner
> —hit or hurt anyone—physically or emotionally—to get my way
>
> I SHALL:
> —seek help when I feel moved to the point of violence
> —speak out when I witness abuse by others
> —encourage others to take an active stand against violence
> —use my hands for healing not harm

Then we sign our names at the bottom of the card. I find it morally invigorating to have such a card butting up against family photos, credit cards, and other wallet miscellany as a constant reminder of what's truly important in my male quest.

There are further steps to take in the program of deepening men's healthy aggression.

Men have found rubbing our brothers' feet a worthwhile challenge. I also invite men to do palm dances with our hands. Brothers close our eyes, connect palms with those of another man, and then alternately express, via our hands, different human emotions like feeling sad, glad, or mad—one man on the giving end, the other on the receiving side. Again, debriefing follows. These are innovative sensual encounters that stir and expand male bodies and souls.

Dancing with one another is a stretch for most men, so we do it gradually, in unfolding stages. We start modern-style, moving separately in front of one another, occasionally touching, or we folk-dance in lines and circles. Slow dancing comes later, and only for those men for whom it provides comfortable play.

But some mode of dancing consistently proves energizing and evocative for brothering circles. As the African saying goes, "No man dancing ever hurt the ground." Most of the men in our brothering path have incrementally grown same-sex confidence, through first participating in all-church dances back at the home church—that is, intergenerational gambols of children, youth, and adults swaying in trusting circles, parties where anyone can dance with anyone . . . at everyone's own pace.

The key is never to cajole, let alone compel, massages or dances (the right of non-participation is always secure). We aspire to promote exchanges of healthy aggression, not additional violations of manhood. The brothering path challenges men to grow, to expand their comfort zones, but the choices remain theirs. Authentic male intimacy is self-determined and mutually shared as we swim fresh waters on the continuum of social, sensual, and sexual communion.

Moreover, at our men's retreats there are always cooperative games such as Frisbee-throwing, building with Lego blocks, and crawling around on the floor as animals . . . alongside competitive ones from "Simon Says" to basketball to horseshoes. Surely, there are times to play games with scores, but our brothering path majors in furnishing imaginative play options as a counterpoint to the conventional fare available in our overly combative male world.

Competition—when untarnished by either all-out conquest or outright harm—can occasion a holy adventure. We men need the push and pull of robust vying, which, at its finest, is a form of aggressive cooperation. Indeed the Latin root of the word *competition* means "to seek together or with others." This root honors the co-creative power of true competition.

As Zen sports writer Tim Gallwey phrases it: "Healthy competition resembles two bulls butting their heads against each other—both grow stronger and each participates in the development of the other."

Letter from a Minister to a Marine

Perhaps the best way to tackle the intricacies of this radical, oft-slippery, distinction between aggression and violence is by presenting a test case. While my example is imperfect, it's certainly male-focused and the tensions are perennially fresh, particularly as our American government has engaged in full-blown warfare in the Middle East, hurdling aggressive measures of international law and cooperation, then jumping straightaway into "shock and awe" violence.

The star of this narrative piece, Bruce, is one of our very own UU-grown young men. It provides a useful context, I think, from which to wrangle more deeply with the formidable issues at hand. This story rotates between the present and past tenses for a reason. The lessons remain a relevant resource among our young adult males, so I've amplified the letter I wrote Bruce some 10 years ago.

First, some background. One of the benefits of a religious minority such as Unitarian Universalism is that we're small enough to reach out quite accessibly to spiritual kin across the land. A Unitarian Universalist acquaintance from the East Coast had a son in the Marine Corps based at Camp Pendleton, in southern California. This young man went UA ("unexplained absence") after experiencing extreme upset in response to something he saw at the camp. In the throes of considerable personal hell he returned to the Marines, still confused, and, according to his father, in need of Unitarian Universalist ministerial support. There was no fellow recruit, officer, or chaplain at Camp Pendleton who could hear, let alone appreciate, his existential anguish. So I was invited to counsel with him. My visit proved helpful to Bruce and transformative for me.

Bruce is a sensitive, muscular, reserved, yet forthright 19-year-old who for seven years had dreamed of becoming a Marine and following in the footsteps of both his uncle and cousin. He was among the top achievers during basic training, so when he jumped camp, it startled everyone, including his buddies. I think he surprised himself as well.

Bruce represents a brave young man saddled with a tormented soul. He still enjoys the drama and grandeur of Marinehood but has grown to loathe the system. He appreciates the discipline and challenge of military life, yet he's learned an irrevocable truth about himself: he's aggressive, all right, a real aggressive kind of guy, but not prone to violence. Bruce cannot kill.

There's more, lots more. Bruce confided that he's always been an emotionally expressive young man, crying openly as a child and youth. Now his feelings are stuffed under the standard regimen of the Marines. He's starved to give voice to his inner feelings and thoughts. Just prior to formally joining the Marines, Bruce was joyfully involved with a group of 10 pre-schoolers as an assistant teacher. In fact, he said that he has but two pressing goals for the future and, now, neither of them is being a career Marine.

The first dream is to own and manage a gym, with special emphasis on bodybuilding; his second mission in life is teaching pre-school children again. Somehow Bruce hopes to blend these visions in one adult life. I can't remember hearing a 19-year-old male express either of these specific desires, let alone both of them together. But there's no doubt in my mind that Bruce is the kind of person who will realize his dreams. As I said: Bruce is aggressive. Currently, when he isn't agonizing over his status with the Marine Corps, Bruce is dreaming about the pre-schoolers he so dearly loves and whom he left behind for the military.

He told me that these children were like little trees that he was summoned to cultivate, prune, and nourish. Now in the Marines he's being trained to cut down similar, if older, trees, and his soul has been torn in two. He doesn't quite know what to do. He can't just up and quit the Marines, because he's the kind of guy who honors commitments; plus, to get out of his military contract at this stage would require extreme measures. Although trapped in severe conscience-pain, Bruce will not be driven to either suicide or assaulting others.

I reminded Bruce that quitting the Marines was complicated, to be sure, but quitting on his soul, an even tougher move, was ultimately at stake. I asked him to remember the trees: the little trees he was tending back in Michigan, the foreign trees he was being trained to cut down, and the ever-growing tree he represented himself. I gave him my phone numbers, we hugged, lest he need me again, whatever decision he made. You see, Bruce was my spiritual brother, scrunched in an agonizingly holy bind.

When I got back to the car I found myself quivering with deep tears for Bruce, for myself, for our world—for both red-blooded Marines and nonviolent ministers, and for all those countless sojourners conflicted with elements of the warrior and the peacemaker clashing in our consciences. For whereas my pathway on issues of nonviolence and war has been relatively uncomplicated given my temperament, upbringing, and life-choices, the older I grow, the more puzzling it all gets.

I was reminded of the wisdom of that hard-nosed pacifist A. J. Muste, who wrote in 1965 that "those who go into war having seriously thought their way to a decision are on a higher moral level than the smug pacifists who've no notion of the ambiguities and contradictions the decision involves."

And I knew that inside my younger brother Bruce, there was an heroic struggle occurring between profound truths, the call to be a warrior and the call to be a peacemaker—or was it, in fact, the cloudy, muddled summons to be some kind of peaceful warrior or militant guardian?

***

Dear Bruce,

Until the next time we talk face-to-face or over the phone, I want you to know that our lengthy conversation on February 8th was a memorable and powerful one for me. The creative tension in my current life isn't as fresh or consequential as your struggle, but my conscience is strangely restless these days, and I hanker to reveal some of my own pesky paradoxes. So, I hope you'll bear with the Reverend awhile. Here goes, Bruce. My only goal is to be helpful.

From a young age forward I was motored by a peaceful, accommodating personality. Cops and robbers never held much fascination for me. I can't ever remember desiring a Red Ryder rifle for Christmas, although there was a period in my life when I was enthralled with water pistols. And the only time I ever handled or shot a real gun was in a Boy Scout drill during a camp-out. I not only flunked the exercise physically, but emotionally as well. I came away from that excursion fearful that shooting at tin cans might be a warm-up exercise for shooting at animals or humans. I remember feeling weird because other scouts seemed to get a real "bang" out of firing guns.

Even when I played sports, which I did with both fervor and excellence (I'm reminded, Bruce, of your passion for wrestling and weight-lifting), my prime drawback was lack of aggressiveness at "crunch-time." My natural meekness would fade into a kind of unwanted passivity. In a nutshell, I was basically "too gentle to live among the wolves," let alone run with them.

Oh, by the way, none of my close male relatives were war veterans, and due to age and academic status, I always managed to avert conscription. I was too immature, perhaps cowardly as well, to obtain conscientious objector status, although that was clearly what I believed and who I was. No wonder I was such a devoted C.O. counselor during the Vietnam War, helping braver ones than I pursue what my conscience had sidestepped.

Peace activist Walter Wink describes himself thusly: "I don't see myself as a pacifist. I see myself rather as a violent person trying to become nonviolent." On the contrary, Bruce, I view myself as a cowardly type, a sanitized pacifist if you will, on the road toward becoming nonviolent as well. Wink and I dwell at different spots on the continuum; nonetheless, both of us require more creative aggression to reach our mutual destination of forceful nonviolence. How would you describe yourself in this regard?

Bruce, let me say that your resistance to taking another person's life lies at the core of nonviolence. By refusing to kill human beings you're proclaiming the supreme worth of every single individual, not only your compatriots but also your foes as well. To kill is perhaps the height of arrogance. For it means playing God, who alone gives life, and who entrusts it to us to cherish and develop, as a gift received with grateful love. Like those trees you've been talking about.

As Unitarians you and I believe in the sacred dignity of every human *unit*. As Universalists we contend that transformation is *universally* accessible to everyone or to no one. The only salvation worth having includes all brothers and sisters, known and foreign, pleasant or unruly, buddies or foes.

Nonviolence is a philosophy, Bruce, which, although infrequently heralded or honored in America, is as old as history itself. From ancient times to the present, people have renounced violence as a means of resolving disputes. They've opted instead for aggressive negotiation, mediation, and reconciliation, resisting violence with an uncompromising respect for the integrity of all human beings, friends and enemies alike.

Examples abound of successful nonviolent action, both here and abroad. Some are well known, others not. Naturally, there's Gandhi's struggle against the British for Indian self-determination as well as the successful nonviolent campaign that won independence for the West African nation of Ghana in 1958. During the Second World War, nonviolent resistance to the Nazis took such forms as the refusal of Norwegian teachers to follow Nazi edicts and the smuggling of Jews from occupied Europe by peacemakers including our own Unitarians, whose bravery launched the work of the Unitarian Universalist Service Committee. And currently in Eastern Europe many of the remarkable revolutionary changes have been accomplished nonviolently.

Bruce, this isn't the way our predominantly blood-and-guts history books read, but if these facts are unknown or obscured, it's only because we've seen fit to interpret the flow of human events largely in terms of the clash of arms. As one unwilling to kill another human being, I want you to know, Bruce, you don't stand alone; rather, you stand in a long and proud tradition—the heritage of nonviolence. And you aren't the first, nor will you be the last man to agonize passionately and painfully with your conscience as a Marine.

Every "real man" must wrestle, Bruce, with what Gandhi called *satyagraha*, which roughly translates as "soul or truth force." The operative word, Bruce, *force*, has been a word which yours truly, frequently hiding out in sweetness or chickenheartedness, has been loathe to claim. But being a resolute, unbending, forceful presence is precisely what is necessary to being truly nonviolent.

Every conflict or problem, whether among family or friends, between communities or governments, or inside your very own conscience, will be addressed ultimately either through violent or nonviolent force. Those who choose nonviolent force opt for the force of justice, the

123

force of love, the force of redistributing power and privilege, the force of noncooperation, the force of relentless resistance to evil, the force of imaginative, revolutionary ideas.

As you can readily see, Bruce, pacifism has nothing in common with passivity or indifference, submission or acquiescence, or even polite compliance. But being tranquil by temperament and conciliatory by conviction, I've had considerable spiritual difficulty, Bruce, in becoming a more tough-minded, stouthearted peacemaker.

In extricating myself from situations of uncomfortable, nasty strife, whether interpersonal, communal, or global, I can all too easily become a smug, self-righteous ideologue—serenely mouthing peaceful platitudes, far removed from the raging battles of reality. Sometimes my resistance to burgeoning, obstinate evils has been so passive that no one has noticed I was resisting, because I wasn't. I was wearing cowardice in disguise.

What I'm urging in a nutshell, Bruce, is for you to be brave, not spineless, and aggressive, not violent.

While we're at it, Bruce, let's wrestle a bit with another thorny concept that the Marines talk a lot about, namely, warrior. The term "warrior" is sullied, perhaps irredeemable, what with its history of paid soldiers whose sole mission is to find and destroy opposition. Usually in our modern world, when the word "warrior" is spoken into existence, war is spoken into existence as well.

Yet in current women's and men's sacred literature, a compelling interpretation of the warrior archetype denotes those individuals who are fiercely compassionate, protectors of righteousness, bold adventurers, boundary-setters, guardians of goodness. For example, Greenpeace, the activist coalition of environmentalists, insistently promotes its mission through "Rainbow Warriors."

Warrior energy, at its healthiest, aggressively protects, builds, and pushes toward humane possibilities. Yet if disconnected from compassion, the warrior can surely become the tool of either a sadist or a masochist and be driven by a passion for cruelty. Its shadow side is exemplified in any governmental, religious, business, or military warlords who use their power to abuse and destroy.

124

Therefore, on the one hand, I remain ready to retire the concept of warrior until we've shown a willingness, for example, to dismantle nuclear weapons worldwide. Yet, on the other hand, I know, Bruce, that in my efforts to approximate justice and combat wrongs I need greater determination, more aggressiveness.

When you spoke to me, Bruce, about your adamant desire to reach your two future goals, I sensed within you an intense, powerful soul activated by what many would call mature warrior strength. Your rigorous goal-setting temperament has assisted as well in your developing an affirmative, healthy flow of aggression. It has also helped immeasurably that your parents are such strong, loving forces in your support-circle.

But lest I place all the so-called "good guys" in the non-military camp, I want you know that in your own heritage of Unitarian Universalism, there have been "warriors" or brave champions within our American military establishment. Did you know that the secretary of defense under President Bill Clinton, Republican Bill Cohen from Maine, is an active Unitarian Universalist layman? Cohen happens to be a very introspective man who writes poetry and, yes, has been working to master the mysteries of the Pentagon. Cohen reminds us that in Chinese and Vietnamese culture, the generals and warriors, as well as political leaders, were often poets.

What I'm driving at, Bruce, is that it's too naive to stereotype military leaders as being violence-mongers. Some are and some aren't. And to complicate matters, I've known my share of public pacifists who were physically abusive at home.

Again I confess, my friend, that truth is stubbornly complex, yet I beckon you to dwell in its messy midst, as you valiantly sculpt a life of holy aggression.

Bruce, I perceive there to be three general responses to evil: passivity, violent opposition, and nonviolence. And if nonviolence doesn't immediately change the heart of the oppressor, it does change the heart of the oppressed, granting new self-respect to the beleaguered. The carrier of nonviolence is also blessed in the process. Nonviolence is the third way, the alternative of Jesus, and it invariably demands that we be imaginative of heart—facing conflicts faithfully rather than fighting or fleeing.

"Nonviolence," said farm-worker activist Cesar Chavez, "forces one to be creative. When people are involved in something constructive, trying to bring about change, they tend to be less violent than those who are not engaged in rebuilding or in anything creative." Aggressive non-violence, I'm convinced, Bruce, is simply more revolutionary than reactive violence, because it draws upon the deepest wellsprings of our human ingenuity and compassion.

Nonviolence invites us to find inventive alternatives beyond violence, to seize the moral initiative, to assert our own humanity and dignity as people, to discover inner resources of power we didn't know we had, to break the cycle of humiliation with ridicule or humor, to refuse to submit or to accept the inferior position, to expose the injustice of the dominator system, to stand our ground, to be willing to suffer rather than retaliate, to force the oppressor to see us in a new light, to be willing to undergo the penalty of breaking unjust laws. Nothing soft or feeble about those actions!

But, Bruce, if you pursue the nonviolent path, you'll inevitably run into those who articulate "but what if . . ." scenarios. Arguments against nonviolence are often about impossible situations where violence wouldn't work either. There is considerable irony in the presumed compassion of a questioner who is so concerned about the potential rape of a single grandmother but also accepts war, in which the rape of grandmothers, wives, daughters, and children is so routine that many soldiers have regarded it as one of the compensations of warfare.

And, Bruce, yes, there are situations that are crushingly tragic, where nothing we can conceivably do will help. Holding hands and singing "Give peace a chance" sometimes doesn't stop warlords from stealing food from starving babies. There are woeful binds when the violent and the nonviolent alike are forced to suffer the agony of irrelevance and may themselves reside among the victims. This is happening even as I write you, throughout the world, in places such as Ireland and the Middle East.

Furthermore, there is nothing magical about nonviolence. It requires courage and hard work, strategizing, self-discipline, and a well-integrated spirituality. It entails willingness to learn from our enemies. It demands the ability to desire their safety as well as our own, to love the part in them that tries to hurt others, even while we refuse to cooperate with it.

126

And no matter how nonviolent we purport to be in theory or practice, we must never envision evil as if it were something arising outside
ourselves. We must confess our complicity in the very evils we abhor. So,
beware, Bruce, of self-righteousness, as you struggle with your conscience
to stay in or leave the Marines.

And remember, Bruce, that nonviolence starts at home. All our phi-
losophizing, important as it is, means nothing unless you and I dare to be
peacemakers, first and foremost, within our own hearts and within our
own households.

In closing, Bruce, your final allegiance must be paid not to the
Marines or to our shared religious heritage or even to your parents, but to
an innermost voice that stays truthful to yourself and loving to the greater
universe. And, above all, my friend, be patient with and kind to yourself,
knowing there's no decision that you can make, however honest, brave,
and compassionate, that will prove pure or stress-free.

I remain your buddy in the common struggle to be peaceful warriors,
to be carriers of "truth-force" all our days on this one, precious Earth.

Your soul-brother,

Tom

Chapter 6: Becoming Elders

Let us take care of the children, for they've a long way to go.
Let us take care of the elders, for they've come a long way.
Let us take care of those in between, for they're doing the
work.

—African prayer

Male Menopause Is Real

Jed Diamond, in his groundbreaking, exhaustively researched book entitled *Male Menopause* (1997), demonstrates that this condition of men is far more than a mid-life crisis. Male menopause is a profound medical, psychological, and emotional reality for millions of men and the people who love them. Actual sons, fathers, and brothers grow increasingly susceptible to irritability and mood swings. As Diamond puts it: "Men at midlife often experience the loss of power, passion, potency, and purpose."

Yet if you're a pre–40-year-old male reading this chapter, someone who's yet to reach what would be labeled mid-life, please don't leave the room or shelve the book. Now's the very time to read this segment with an open heart and compassionate vision, because it's written specifically to prepare your body and soul for what lies ahead. Younger guys need to think of aging not as a disease but as a series of negotiable passages, often a bridge to brighter and more beautiful things.

Indeed, as I compose the following sentiments, I'm holding close in my heart our own two sons, Chris and Russ, as well as our son-in-law, Jaya, who are 42, 35, and 30 respectively. I want these dear young men to take seriously Abraham Lincoln's words: "A man is responsible for his own face after forty." I want them, as necessary, to rethink, even reinvent, their lives in order to neutralize sameness and sourness. I want our adult "boys" to experience abundant honor and hope as they journey toward elderhood. In short, I desire that Chris, Russ, and Jaya, as well as their male contemporaries, might gray as gracefully as possible in their allotted days and nights.

One of our Unitarian Universalist brothers in his 40s, upon learning that I was doing a workshop on this theme of "Graying Gracefully," said: "Whoa, I've been counting on life beginning at 50, not ending there. I've understood that everything up until the graying years is training, and it's in the 50–65 year age range that we want to take all we've learned and make our true mark on the world. Given this, I hope your talk and work-shop will focus upon rejuvenation into what would ideally be my most alive years yet."

And I responded: "Feelings noted, my brother. I'll do what I can."

Furthermore, it's only fair to launch with a snapshot of my own aging condition. I've just completed full-time ministerial service of 35 years, and, while I'm not formally retired, I will presumably play and vol-unteer more than consult and work in the days ahead. At least that's my plan, but passion and money have a way of derailing things, so my soul remains wide-open to life's shifting winds. I usually tell people "I've just commenced, not retired. I'm transitioning into a new chapter of my evolving tale."

How do things feel from my present perch? Well, my body's full of weird aches and ailments. My runs are shorter, actually more like fast walks. All my physical drives are waning. Strange stuff's growing on my body. And I resonate with the view of John Updike, who, at 70, wrote in his most recent novel, *Seek My Face*: "in old age . . . everything wears thin—the skin thins and declares its sun damage, the cartilage thins and bones grind one upon another, the membrane between what one feels and what one says thins."

There's more. I used to be a whiz with names; I'm merely an above-average rememberer now. I'm more desirous of viewing than climbing mountains. I blatantly need and grab more sleep. I'm frustrated more easily. I need people both less and more—a curious state of affairs.

My competitive urges are giving way to contemplative moods. So, although I may enter a tennis tournament or two in the years up ahead, I'm more likely to take up yoga to arouse my sagging spirit and realign my gnarled body. Nearing 62, I'm ready to garner my social security checks as well as grab my share of discounts at movies and restaurants. I'm not shutting down by a long shot, but I'm slowing down.

So, here goes, some ruminations upon the process of men becoming elders, mulched in the soil of my soul. Brothers of all ages, listen in, glean what proves useful, and shuck the rest. And sisters, thanks for picking up this book: I hope there's an observation or two pertinent to your own maturing quest.

Eldering: Yesterday and Today

> The old must live in the young like a grounding force that tames the tendency towards bold but senseless actions and shows them the path of wisdom. In the absence of elders, the impetuosity of youth becomes the slow death of the community.
>
> —Malidoma Patrice Somé

The root of the word *old* means "to nourish." Old age was originally associated with strength, not weakness. As James Hillman observes in *The Force of Character*, "the old were regarded as stable depositories of customs and legends, guardians of local values, experts in skills and crafts, and valued voices in the communal council. What mattered was force of character proven by length of years." Consequently, in the Haida Nation, elders seldom became senile because they were needed right up to the end.

The gray-heads, in ancient times, served as the sacred mentors in their villages, being finally deemed smart and free enough to make significant, enduring contributions. They would sit at the gates of cities imparting wisdom to the younger men. A man among men, the elder was sought after for crucial guidance, nurture, and understanding of life. To sit in the circle of such sages was actually the lifelong pursuit of young men.

To be sure, few of these older guys were particularly brilliant, compassionate, and exemplary, but they had endured the slings and arrows of existence. They were still awake and had earned the right to be heard. The older men needed to open their mouths, and the less experienced ones needed to open their ears. A soulful covenant of speaking-and-listening was struck.

But, in current society, especially in the West, the opposite situation prevails. Our would-be elders are frequently seen playing shuffleboard in parks, watching inane sitcoms at home, hunkering down in retirement homes, medicating themselves out of reality, frantically trying to reverse the inexorable erosions of time, or simply waiting around to close up shop.

There are exceptions, to be sure; not all sages and crones are entrapped, lonely or lost, societal throwaways. There exist a growing number of programs that invite, even employ, our elders in schools, businesses, and community organizations.

We're recognizing now that seniors, unless very frail, are capable of making valuable contributions. They furnish the backbone of our large and growing volunteer economy, where they help out providing abundant public services—education, environmental work, business consultation, and caregiving.

Marc Freedman writes in *Prime Time: How Baby Boomers Will Revolutionize Retirement and Transform America:* "America's burgeoning older population is poised to become the new trustees of civic life in this country." Contrary to the predictions that elders will only drain resources, a growing number of retirees are giving back more than they're taking— and receiving psycho-spiritual nourishment in the process. In a study of "Leaps in Literacy," 94% of older volunteers report having grown personally through their tutoring with children, and 83% said they felt more connected to the community. Clearly, the benefits are cross-generational.

But let's not get carried away. On the whole, rarely do we see senior men being the "grounding force" in American society that African spiritual guide Malidoma Somé urges. How many men can you name making things with little boys or engaged in meaningful discourse with the younger turks? In our own extended families or church communities, let alone in the greater society?

This poses not only a personal problem but a social one as well. Our aging men are frequently disregarded and despondent, saddled with a succession of poverties: of financial means, of energy and achievement, of motivation, and saddest of all, poverty of hope and affection.

Aging can make men psychologically more vulnerable, brittle, and prone to self-destruction. By age 60 the rate for successful suicides is at least five times as high for men as for women. Also, men of 60 or older kill themselves at rates approximately four times greater than men under 20. Clearly, for too many males, seniority doesn't deliver security, wisdom, serenity, mellowness, and philosophical acceptance.

Contemporary elders need assistance and support.

The Church Exists to Serve Its Gray-Heads

How will our global community evolve sustainable social and spiritual structures for an aging population? Did you know there are now an estimated 629 million people in the world age 60 and over? By 2050, that number is projected to grow to almost 2 billion, and—for the first time in human history—the world will have more people 60 and over than children under age 15.

Are not seniors real, live folks with continuing needs to forgive and be forgiven, to deepen and broaden their journeys as long as they breathe? Is there any holier task for a religious community to assume than enabling our sages and crones to complete their jaunts with as much generativity and integrity as possible? Is that not the mission of a church, mosque, sangha, or temple: being a center of redemption and renewal that helps our gray-heads stay vital until the grave?

Even as we peruse our own liberal religious ranks, we take those in their 60s and above grossly for granted. We either assume they'll keep on doing what they've always done or we infer that, due to waning energy, they can't do much of anything anymore, so we stop asking them. Let them be, let them go, let them fade . . . away. Across the board we pay less and less attention to our aging and aged brothers and sisters.

One man in his home congregation was a full-fledged leader for over four decades. Charles had more than paid his dues. He was a consummate *steward*—literally a "keeper of the hall"—during fair and foul weather.

But when Charles progressed from being a well-aging to an ill-elderly man, and couldn't attend church much any more, he was dropped like a hot potato. Less vital and less visible than in his heyday, Charles was basically forgotten, not due to mean-spirited intention, but simply lack of consistent attention. Although there was an established caregiving committee, Charles somehow got lost in the cracks.

As he put it: "Just when I needed my church the most, it wasn't there for me!" But Charles didn't quit; that wasn't his way. Nonetheless, he suffered.

That's a story that could be retold in every one of our Unitarian Universalist congregations across the land. I recount it not to make laity and religious professionals feel guilty but to motivate us to be aggressive caregivers, with all ages of members, from start to finish. As our babies need our regular, caring touch, so do our seniors.

One of the earliest, and most influential, motivations for my entrance into ministry was accompanying our pastor, when I was a pre-teenager, while he made house and hospital calls to seniors. And later on in my actual ministry, I've invariably come away from interactions with elders feeling that I've just experienced the most privileged and sacred of connections.

One of my aspirations, as my life unfolds after full-time work, is to return to the primal source of my call: to visit elders, in their places of residence, building authentic, affectional bonds through touch and song, conversation and games. I will arrive neither as pastor nor family member but as human kin. I want to assist them in living more creatively, lovingly, and serenely during their homestretch. In blessing them, I will be blessed in return.

Our seniors sorely need external prods and nudges to keep their engines running. Especially the men, who've lived lives of rugged independence and who are less adept, although just as hungry, at navigating social communion. I'll be doing this out of duty and joy but also because of enlightened self-interest; for I'm aging too, and want to keep in vital spiritual shape as a late junior fast becoming an early senior.

After all, I'll shortly be their peer, numbered among the sages, perhaps dwelling in their midst, not just visiting. And I'm not embarrassed or chagrined to confess that I'll covet the touch and sight and words of some of the younger folks reading this book, even as you'll someday need the brothers coming along after you.

Ways to Honor Our Sages

Legion are the reasons why we fail our elders: we're squeamish around them; we're frightened of our own graying; we loathe seeing vital people decline; or we've got to build our church around the givers, not the takers; or you name it. There are plenty of explanations, but none good enough to excuse abandonment of our sages and crones.

Caring about seniors shouldn't wait until they're housebound. We've got to start the honoring process much earlier. What if we launched a bridging celebration of some substance for our elders when they reach age 60, thanking them for their savvy and service and liberating them to participate in fresh ways during the golden years? Our churches currently schedule bridging ceremonies for almost every other era-of-passage: for babies, for coming of age youth, for young adults. Why not foster programs and rites explicitly for our seniors?

If we want our elders to celebrate, not merely tolerate, their final years, this will require special attention from our beloved communities. Again, are not our churches the places where deep, durable confirmation of men must transpire at every stage, from birth to death? We abdicate this responsibility at grave cost to our individual and institutional souls.

Rev. Nancy Arnold from our Akron, Ohio church, in collaboration with lay leaders, has inaugurated a *Circle of Elders*, where one must be at least 60 years old, a member of the church for 20 or more years, and have demonstrated over the course of membership a strong involvement in the ongoing work of the church. These folks are recognized and respected for their leadership, promotion, and support of their chosen parish. Like elders in the Native American tradition, they, in turn, are asked to advise the chiefs and teach the children, since they have more time than the younger generation. As this congregation puts it:

> Traditionally, in the West, men were asked to be Elders; in the East, it was the women. Since we're in the Midwest, we will draw from both men and women when choosing the Elders in our church. Each one passes on a bit of wisdom from their life experience to the younger generations. This way, the wisdom is carried from one generation to the next, and the circle of life experience is not broken.
>
> There's an ancient Hindu proverb that says, "Don't cut down the wisdom tree." In our western culture, the elders are not seen as valuable and wise. Youth and vital energy are elevated at the expense of anyone who is not young and healthy. Our UU tradition teaches us to value all ages; hence, we must draw from the wisdom of all ages.

In San Diego, we've occasioned long-standing croning ceremonies for women (55 years of age and above) and are developing equally relevant and cherished rites for saluting the sages in our ranks. No flawless ways exist to recognize our elders, so congregations must experiment and explore modes that are satisfying to partakers. The need is long overdue—truly, of increasing urgency. As the Nike ad exhorts: Just do it!

Our Men's Fellowship has honored our senior brothers in a potpourri of venues. We ensure that every panel discussion of men includes an elder's perspective. And periodically, sometimes planned and other times spontaneously, we invite our elders to stand or sit in the middle of our entire brothering community. Then, for a few moments, the outer contingent of men affirms the innate worth and stature of the older men—showering them with chants, kudos, and caresses. The elders aren't allowed to respond or reciprocate; they're mandated to soak in the gratitude. They're solely blessed.

On other occasions we invite our elders to dwell in the midst of the circle and face outward toward the younger men. This time they're encouraged to speak their pieces, each for several minutes. Our older kin voice past aches, current passions, and future hopes. Or we schedule times for the younger men to solicit from the elders lessons pertinent to their specific age: 17 or 25 or 40 or 55. And the gathered sages reflect back upon what they knew and didn't know at 17 or 25 or 40 or 55.

There's palpable hunger both for the elders to transmit their hard-won wisdom and for the youngers to receive it. A full-fledged blessing transpires as tales are told of fierce storms and tamed tigers, grievous losses and wondrous highs. At our conferences, whatever the overall theme might be (ranging from ending men's violence to reclaiming our bodies to deep playfulness to becoming earth stewards to finding our life's call), there's always sacred time set aside for elder-younger communion.

Younger and Older Men Save Each Other

> If you're not being admired by an older man, you're being hurt; if you're an older man and you're not being admired by a younger man, you're being hurt.
>
> —Robert Moore

I'm not sure how much actual blessing-and-being-blessed occurs for men at workstations, during home lives, or in fraternal organizations. My measured observation is: not enough, and what there is doesn't travel deeply enough. Therefore, the main load of spiritual eldering needs to be carried by our religious tribes. And why not? We're intentionally built to foster deep brothering.

Now, brothering doesn't have to be structured as formal mentoring, although that's vitally needed in our culture. Just having older and younger men together—eating and sleeping, hiking and conversing, drumming and singing, dancing and weeping—for weekends in the mountains or evenings in the church parlor delivers soul-stretching camaraderie.

My buddy George, now in his 70s, an active member of our San Diego Men's Fellowship for years, went on to cultivate the brothering vineyards in Canada. He's currently summing up his life by writing vignettes, principally for his four boys, assorted other relatives, and friends. George relates that definitive studies have shown that men who experience the most successful old ages with respect to health, happiness, and comfort, possess in common one major criterion: *regular involvement with people younger than they are.*

Psychologist Erik Erikson talks about the major challenges for our mature years being affiliation, generativity, and ego-integrity. All three are met when seniors and juniors interact meaningfully with visits, talks, projects, and embraces.

Younger men are invariably fed by the sagacity of their older brothers: wisdom that includes travesties as well as triumphs, interspersed with tons of hard-earned comebacks. They flourish in being blessed. And the elders ripen in being able to bless younger guys, who, after all, will be inheriting the earth after the graybeards are gone.

Tears flow from all corners of the room in these salvational exchanges. The elders are saved by being affirmed; the youngers are saved by being fed. And vice versa. The saving flows in both directions.

Former vice-president Hubert Humphrey, nearing death, addressed Congress with these profound sentiments: "The true, moral test of a country is what we do with those at the *dawn* of life (our children), those enduring the *shadows* of life (our oppressed), and those entering the *twilight* of life (our elders)." Sound doctrine indeed!

Senior after senior moans about how we lose our primary identity and value when we stop working or producing. But our worth is regained through intergenerational rituals and encounters. Why? Because we feel accepted for our innate personhood, not our measured productivity. Elders need to feel validated for our past, confirmed for who we are now, and knighted for unimagined sacred ventures ahead. Senior men come to our retreats, locked in procrustean beds of denigrating labels such as "old farts" and "old geezers"; they leave liberated as elders.

Brother Michael spoke for many gray-heads when he wept with joy in telling us:

At our Men's Renewal weekend, being able to bless some of you guys alongside you blessing me in return stands as a highlight of my life. We've just shared what I never got growing up as a boy, never risked in my young adult years, and never expected during the twilight years. Thanks to this incomparable time of blessing and being blessed. I can now proudly walk off into the woods and complete my journey. It's enough. I'm done now. Keep the blessings flowing!

Michael died within the year. At peace with himself and his Creator.

Men Blessing and Being Blessed

My fiftieth year had come and gone,
I sat a solitary man,
In a crowded London shop,
An open book and empty cup
On the marble table-top.
While on the shop and street I gazed
My body of a sudden blazed;
And twenty minutes more or less
It seemed, so great my happiness,
That I was blessed and could bless.

—William Butler Yeats

Upon turning 50, the Irish bard W. B. Yeats penned this forceful poem about blessing and being blessed by the world. He actually phrased it: "that I was blessed and could bless," which, in truth, captures the proper spiritual order. Creation blesses us, then we return the favor. Humans don't initiate the blessing process; we merely ignore or confirm it. Nonetheless, I want to start with *doing*, our male proclivity, then close with *being*, a tougher charge.

The genius of Yeats's admonition is that it challenges men to mature both as givers and receivers. Evolving manhood is not equatable with either the passive tone of quietude or the activist demeanor of proficiency. Eldering requires both in cadenced measure.

I exhort men of 50 and above to be bilateral, to move ambidextrously and agilely between both blessing and being blessed as we saunter down life's lane. In fact, that's a recommendable life-rhythm for all adult males. Mature liberal religious masculinity, the mission of the brothering quest, is quintessentially about balance. As Carl Jung summed it up: "The definition of maturity is holding greater and greater opposites without coming apart."

Maintaining equilibrium is an essential skill for aging men, since we're prone to vault out of kilter, incognizant of the need to square "being still and still moving," as T. S. Eliot puts it. One of my prized art possessions is a weighty bronze sculpture created by Carol Gold, entitled *Equilibrio*—in Spanish, the "balancing one."

On the desk in my study stands this robust male figure, one arm thrust outward for intimacy, the other upward in yearning. The left leg is lifted; the right one is planted firmly on the narrow, precarious path of life. *Equilibrio* visually depicts the balancing act of the brother-spirit quest, in which men are charged to maintain equipoise between the various enticements of existence: spirit and body, friendship and solitude, desire and wound, work and play, poetry and politics, descent into earth and ascent into the heavens, hermitage and knightly endeavor, fierceness and tenderness. As well as blessing and being blessed. *Equilibrio*, the balancer, gazes inward for strength without falling into the dizzying depths of the abyss. Responsive, courageous, awake elders are summoned to walk this rail.

Seniors need to be just as balanced physically, emotionally, and spiritually as little boys, young men, and midlifers do. Naturally, the age-appropriate tasks are different for 10- or 30- or 50- or 70- or 90-year-old males, but the quest for equilibrium is everlasting. Elder energy produces and yields, serves and surrenders.

Growing old is arguably the most arduous passage we humans navigate, a mixed blessing to be sure. But men can un-mix it some if we become versatile in our blessing efforts. Whether giving or receiving, brothers can fulfill one of my favorite scriptures on maintaining an evergreen awareness: "In old age they still produce fruit; they are always green and full of sap" (Psalm 92:14).

Our perpetual goal in aging is not perfection but completion, finishing well. Our final laps as men should be ones in which we still produce fruit, utterly "green and full of sap,"—but not primarily through performing or producing. It's tough for men to be still and feel adequate, to be full of sap . . . sitting, without directing or marshaling anything or anyone . . . just being quiet, letting go of outcomes, and allowing the sap to drip. I am reminded of the stanza from a fine Jane Kenyon poem:

> Let it come as it will, and don't
> Be afraid. God does not leave us
> Comfortless, so let evening come.

Erik Erikson says the final life-crisis revolves around "integrity versus despair." Well, integrity means displaying wholeness and embodying dignity during our closing laps. To do and be so, men will need to live alternately as givers and receivers: blessing and being blessed.

Blessing

> We need to shift from aging to saging, which entails acting as guide, mentor, and agent of healing and reconciliation on behalf of the planet, nation, tribe, clan, and family—becoming wisdom keepers.
>
> —Rabbi Zalman Schachter-Shalomi

Let's first view men in the active voice, the mode of blessing.

Elders are consciously engaged in life, harvesting all the way home, developing character, unwilling to disappear during life's third act. We track Shakespeare's wisdom: "This is to be new born when thou art old, to see thy blood warm when thou feels't it cold." Sages keep our embrace wide open. We exude "the gift of intelligent rage," knowing what things to fight and what things to disregard. I offer three ways to remain in the active voice, in order to be a blesser of the Creation: serving others, taking risks, and grandfathering. You could readily name others.

Serving Others

> And if I ever touched a life, I hope that life knows that
> I know that touching was and still is and will always be
> the true revolution.

—Nikki Giovanni

First, elders refuse to narcoticize ourselves with medicine or idleness and instead focus on interests of note and challenges of substance. Bingo may suffice as an intermittent diversion but not as a fulfilling activity for elders. One of the ways men stay vital is by undertaking tasks of worth—not to earn money or applause but to enhance our souls.

The key thing to remember is that nobody, at any age, ever finds life worth living, but, as minister Harry Emerson Fosdick used to say: "One always has to *make* it worth living by an interior, creative, spiritual contribution of one's very own." Elders have lived long enough to know that worthwhileness isn't found in a book, or under a rock, or in a foreign land. You don't get it from gurus, gold, or even gods. You make life worth living. You reach out and truly touch existence, to paraphrase Nikki Giovanni.

In the years ahead, I plan to continue to make my life valuable by assisting those on both ends of the age spectrum, children and seniors, to become more visible and audible. I hope to tutor children in schools and coach little leaguers. As an elder-volunteer I want more hands-on connection and less overall accountability.

And as I noted earlier, I also plan to enter nursing homes and sing to and with those in their 70s to 90s, reclaiming melodies of yesteryear in order to induce a bounce in their step and some spark in their eyes. I'll take my older life-companions on walks around the block, play zany, non-competitive physical games, and perform magic tricks. My goal is to keep their motors running (mine too) by being an unabashed joy-bringer. From here on out, my card will read—and my character will reflect— *merry-maker*.

We elders would do well to grow in alignment with the prayerful challenge of Dwight Judy in order for our masculine spirit to contribute toward transforming society:

> Send me into the village square, send me into the schools, send me into the day camps for children, send me into the task of creating beauty, send me into the business world to create more jobs, send me into the political world to struggle for the values I hold dear, send me into the earth as her son, to love her and to cherish her. Send me to help create the "thousand healths and hidden isles" not even yet imagined. Amen.

May it come to pass; may we men be integral partners in serving a vision that will enable such a just and joyous world to be born.

Taking Risks

> Be patient with yourself. You're growing brain. That's literally true. If you continually introduce new learning situations and put yourself at some risk, even an older, developed brain can sprout new foliage and make new neural connections.
>
> —Gail Sheehy

To be sure, we need to keep growing our brains, for growth is evidence of life. A veteran American poet was asked how he kept young in spirit, and he pointed to the cherry tree in blossom, asking in turn, "Where are the blossoms?" The answer was "On the new wood." It's the young branches that have the blossoms and bear fruit. Elders, like trees, keep on going by growing new life.

The Canadian novelist Robertson Davies claimed that the finest gift we can exhibit during our senior years is curiosity: "Curiosity about something. Enthusiasm. Zest. That's what makes old age a delight. One has seen so much yet is eager to see more. You're not getting older, you're getting nosier." Or as I would put it: when we're young, we yield to noisiness; when we're older, we're unleashed to focus on nosiness!

Furthermore, while life may be more uncertain and health less stable, expectations and pressures are lifted in our saging years so we can become curious—nay, brazen—adventurers. We've earned the right to be freer and fiercer. Elders can venture tasks without specific purpose, yet laden with great meaning. Chances can be taken now that we didn't risk earlier, because we've less to lose—certainly not promotions or even adulation. Taking risks means removing our armor, or, as a male friend vividly puts it: "elderhood is the time to dismantle our vertical coffins."

When we retire (or "graduate from work" as one teenager mused), it's the season to re-tire, as in "put on new treads." It's an exceptional opportunity to explore innovative realities—perhaps gardening around church grounds, tutoring in prisons, taking up bird watching, or joining the Peace Corps as one brother did.

I love the playful exchange in Lewis Carroll's *Alice in Wonderland*:

"You are old, Father William," the young man said,
"And your hair has become very white;
And yet you incessantly stand on your head—
Do you think, at your age, it is right?"

"In my youth," Father William replied to his son,
"I feared it might injure the brain;
But now that I'm perfectly sure I have none,
Why, I'd do it again and again."

Elders are, at long last, more willing to venture upside-down attitudes and behaviors because we're less worried about the world's judgment or, alas, even our own brains.

Last fall, elder Cliff Kindy, an organic farmer from Indiana who once made a pilgrimage to South America to stand up to Colombian rebels, led a 10-day anti-war delegation to Iraq of about a dozen senior citizens from the United States and Canada. Kindy figured his intrepid venture might force the Bush administration to think twice about attacking or invading Iraq. "You get about 500 grandmas and grandpas from around the world and you scatter them around Iraq, as human shields, and dare the U.S. to bomb them. That would give us some collective moral authority."

I exhort all elders to consider a similar bold directive in which to become a blessing. Our own peculiar blessing. Work in a shelter serving meals as Pete and Oscar do. Travel with police cars at night through the streets of your city, to serve and protect society, as Hosea does. Be imaginative, be adventurous, and serve in ways you've been waiting all your days to do. Now's the time.

Grandfathering

God is still imaged by the majority of Westerners as an old white man. Yet the tragic irony is that elderly white guys are hardly revered, let alone valued, in our culture. I only have to turn to the three old men on my side of the family, Frank and John, my grandfathers and Harold, my dad. Their mature years were not that mature, let alone happy or useful. I seriously doubt if any of these men felt they met Yeats's standard for fulfillment: blessing and being blessed.

Since our first grandchild, Trevor, was born some seven years ago, I've given lots of tear-soaked thoughts to the grandfathering enterprise in particular, and its eldering relevance. This section cross-qualifies as elderhood in both its active and passive voices, for grandfathering is definitely a door that swings in and out, back and forth, blessing and being blessed.

My grandfathers John Joseph Flanagan and Frank Wilber Towle are buried in my marrow, sprouting now and again in the movements of my own body and mind.

John Joseph and I were both born on October 13th. He was a quiet, gentle man who displayed keen responsibility for his entire clan. He was a leader who possessed a strong sense of fairness and concern for others. John was a lover of fun, hard working, and handsome. Sorta like me!

Frank Wilber was born in Lawrence, Massachusetts and grew up an Easterner. I've always wondered why a native Californian like myself could feel a visceral connection with the East Coast, and I think it must be because of him. He was an intellectual, always studying this or that while the weeds grew up around him. Frank could have been a college professor, but that path just didn't materialize. Instead he became a music teacher of the banjo, mandolin, and guitar. Those passions turned up in my genes as well.

Frank Wilber never joined any religion but is reported to have had an attraction to Unitarianism and Unitarianism alone. My father, once after hearing a sermon of mine, wistfully remarked: "This was right down your grandfather's alley. He would have understood it, agreed with it, been moved by it. He would have joined your church. I wish he could have heard his grandson preach!" So do I.

Frank and John are my blood-and-spirit brothers. They gave birth to me. I carry their seed forward. We dwell inside one another, despite the fact that I never knew them. You see, John and Frank died before I was born, one of a heart attack, all too young; the other by his own hand, all too sad.

In the nine months leading up to our first grandchild Trevor's birth, I possessed a heartful of growing delight and niggling anxiety—*delight* because I would be the beneficiary of precious time with a tiny baby, something I didn't share enough of in my own parenting. *Anxiety*, because I never benefited firsthand from a grandfathering presence, so I was nervous about being one myself.

My befuddled sentiments were reflected in the journal jitters I composed early on in our daughter-in-law Misha's pregnancy. "I never knew my grandfathers. Can I be one? How will I be one? Whom can I follow, whom can I resemble? Well, whatever you try, shun comparisons with award-winning grandpas, and, above all else, as tempted as you'll be— beware of atoning for all you failed to accomplish as a father. Put aside dreams of grandeur or being grand and just be the fullest grown man you are next to Trevor being the fullest baby boy he is. Nothing you can DO will ever be enough anyway, yet everything you simply ARE will strangely prove a gift!"

146

Squarely facing my fears in preparation for Trevor's arrival, then writing them down privately, seemed to steady me.

By the way, did you know that the word *grandfather* in rabbinical Hebrew means "my old person, my sage" and that Naomi says in the Book of Ruth: "The grandchild shall be to you a restorer of your soul and will sustain your old age?" I like the balance, and I've come to envision grandfathering as my challenge to be one source of *wisdom* for young Trevor along the way while welcoming him as a *restorer* of my soul in return. Quite a satisfying deal, if you ask me.

I could not have expected, despite my raw sentimentalist nature, the fountain of warm tears that flowed when I held Trevor for the first time on his day of birth. Somehow I knew instantaneously that a bedrock affection, both of and beyond my making, would prove sufficient to transcend my trepidations and inadequacies. When I held him on his natal day, and every time I've held him since, I experience a strange yet gratifying assurance that he and I, not blood-kin, will find our ways to become soul-kin.

Of course, there are no guarantees, only opportunities, in this adventure called grandparenting. The situations vary widely in our culture, and each connection must be honored in its peculiar specialness. Some of us are able to enjoy an active presence in our grandchild's life. A few of us are even raising our grandchildren. Others are distant geographically or emotionally from either our children or grandchildren. None of us can judge, or fully empathize with, the grandfathering challenges experienced by another elder.

The best I can manage is to shelve my vast array of worldly wisdom and simply be present to, for, and with this unique, irrepeatable child named Trevor, who will call me Grandpa or some version thereof the rest of my days. Can I learn to keep my heart open and my mouth quiet? Can we simply walk hand in hand and experience the wonder of the world together?

Although Trevor will never look like me, perhaps he will someday sound a bit like me as he makes his own way through existence. Surely, our respective smells will never be forgotten, which is, after all, what I recall most vividly about the intimacy with my own father: the unmistakable aroma of his cheeks.

I didn't produce Trevor; I didn't produce the child that was involved in producing Trevor. But, although biologically removed, I'm emotionally involved as one presence among eight grandparents and countless other companions in this little traveler's journey. And, along the pathway, Trevor will somehow learn that while he isn't the whole of my world, when I'm right next to him, he is the designated center of my universe.

Being Blessed

No duties. I don't have to be profound.
I don't have to be artistically perfect.
Or sublime. Or edifying.
I just wander . . .
And now the music of the worlds transforms me.
My planet enters a different house.
Let others take care of it. Time for me to pay hooky.
Buena notte. Ciao. Farewell.

—Czeslaw Milosz
(composed in 1991 when Milosz
was 80 years old)

In the Christian scriptures some men reportedly come to Jesus and want to know what they must do to inherit the kingdom of God (Mark 5:36 and 10:21). Much to their amazement and consternation, Jesus responds that it won't take *doing* but *being* something. Unfortunately, the men turn aside and amble off.

I share with Carl Jung the conviction that the second half of one's life has primarily to do with the exploration of one's spiritual being. "Among my patients in the second half of life . . . there has not been one whose problem in the last resort was not that of finding a religious outlook on life. . . ."

In the first half of life, men are developing outreach, going forth to make good in the world, rear children, and care for others. "But

148

whoever carries over into the afternoon the aims of the morning must pay for it with damage to the soul," says Jung. Consequently, in the second half, adult males need to search within—to know life more deeply, to know our ultimate destiny to fulfill. What Jung calls the "religious outlook."

However, this gradual move away from the dominant *doingness* of our earlier years into the *beingness* of the second half of life doesn't mean that elders are committed to *nothingness*. Hardly. Being is a creative, fulsome state in its own right. It takes as much energy, albeit a different kind, to be blessed as it takes to bless. In truth, it may require greater effort, for most men, to soul, shed, and surrender than it does for us to serve and take risks. The salient reminder here is that both conditions are required to be a whole man, a mature brother, and an elder.

My dad, like so many males of his generation, never got the hang of being comfortable in the hands of others. In fact, he died, perhaps purposefully, before caregivers could surround him. Harold Alexander Towle was a man of his times: a consummate provider who plumbed precious little of his inner kingdom.

Dad was able to bless others, here and there, but rarely allowed others truly to bless him. Dad's adult-long vocation was selling insurance, but he pursued no real avocations except playing the guitar and listening to games on the radio, both of which faded somewhat in his latter years. Although I hasten to add that Dad was scheduled to play a New Year's Eve gig the very week after he died.

We talk about today's kids being robbed of their childhoods by parents pushing them into almost non-stop, frenetic activity. But could it be true that our society is similarly robbing seniors of their full elderhood: the glorious, balanced experience of blessing and being blessed?

Dad couldn't sit still, tolerate silence, and surrender to being, just being. He was productive in his own fashion but hardly fulfilled as a man. He deserved better. My dad got older without becoming much of an elder. His heart and spirit grew dim, then his body followed suit.

He kept trudging into the office, continued to sell some insurance, and then a few months shy of 82 years of age, Dad had had enough. He was wearing out; so he went home, mainly, I think, to arrange financial matters for his beloved Mary's future. Within a matter of weeks, he got ill, went to the hospital, and died behind a closed door.

I can't really quarrel with Dad's manner of shutting down and sauntering off, as animals do in the woods, for he knew no other way. But it won't be mine.

If I'm fortunate, I hope to be an elder, a *zaken*, the Hebrew word for "gray-headed"—which I already am, but a gray-head who dares to juggle service and stillness, who will risk adventures that don't have to prove much of anything . . . in short, an older guy who seeks his share of blessing and be blessed.

So, if I'm not mistaken, we've come full circle, for the foundational thesis of this book has been *saving the males*: saving them as boys, saving them as youth, saving them as adults, and, yes, saving them as seniors.

I would propose three modes of salvation related to men permitting ourselves to be blessed. I call them souling, shedding, and surrendering.

Souling

> The Soulful Quest is a pilgrimage into the depths of the self. We leave the sunlit world of easy roles and prefabricated tokens of masculinity, penetrate the character armor, get beneath the personality, and plunge into the chaos and pain of the old masculine self . . . confronting the demons and dark shadows that have held us captive from their underground haunts.
>
> —Sam Keen

The elder realizes that being blessed starts within himself, for if there's ever a decisive time to confirm one's own worthiness, it's during our second adulthood. Being an elder occasions abundant opportunities to be blessed by others as well, but why not start with oneself, by reclaiming one's own peculiar, irrepeatable loveliness? As Poet Galway Kinnell puts it: "for everything flowers, from within, of self-blessing."

Rather than continuing either to submerge yourself or follow some-body else's script (as most men are programmed to do during the bulk of their early- to mid-adult lives), now's the time to say Yes to your one and only true self. Rabbi Zusya was right on target: "At the end of my life, Yahweh won't ask me why I wasn't Moses, but why I wasn't Zusya!"

By mid-life, men are sufficiently familiar with our own peculiar weak-nesses and strengths, our singular ground and sky, so that we can halt tin-kering with our temperament and begin to accept ourselves as we actual-ly are. Moving from mid-life into elderhood is not a time for overhauls but for adjustments.

Mature men believe in growing old as naturally and gracefully as pos-sible. My brows, chin, nose, hair color, wrinkles, blemishes, and nicks—my face is mine. Not always happy, frowning when necessary, seldom hid-ing when in view, may it be a faithful face, one that reveals my genuine feelings and one that can be met head-on.

Authentic self-blessing requires traveling inside, descending deep within the soul. The majority of modern adult men are relatively unfa-miliar with their inner terrain, for we've lived mostly above ground, in the sunlight, if not limelight—rising, climbing, and progressing. But mid-life and beyond constitutes the season to slow down, saunter not race, brood, "rake the ashes" as Bly puts it, and deal with our own mortality. Having been sky-dwellers much of our adult lives, men should now prudently revisit the soil from whence we arrived.

Have no illusions, my brothers. Souling will likely unearth some of the nastiest stuff you'll ever tackle, but trust me, if you survive the con-frontation, you'll be profoundly blessed in the process. Elders possess the quality time and emotional elasticity to do this digging. Furthermore, souling is not done in order to report to a boss, confess to a therapist, or even to please God. Souling is ventured fundamentally for oneself, to bring our life toward a sense of greater alignment—the "integrity" to which Erikson refers.

Making sufficient peace with our masculine souls will comprise grap-pling with leftover, often unresolved, *angst, anger,* and *anguish*—those severe blessings of the netherworld. Genuine souling requires more raw courage than acquired knowledge.

151

Suffice it to say, fears dwell in our souls which, if unfaced now, will unnecessarily torment us all the way to our graves. There is bitterness that, left unaddressed, diminishes our being. And there is immense mourning to be done.

Eldering presents men with the challenge neither to forget these potent emotions nor to flee or fight them, but to face them squarely. At this stage in our masculine quest we can confront, and, if we're lucky, transform angst, anger, and anguish into healthful energies for our closing laps.

Souling, at core, will require deep crying.

"And Jesus wept" is the shortest verse in the Christian scriptures, but, oh, what a mighty sentiment—particularly for emotionally constricted older guys teeming with groans, sighs, and tears to be released. Like most modern males at this stage in the journey, Jesus was afraid, enraged, and grieving—that is, full of angst, anger, and anguish.

The Nazarene was distraught over the rotten behavior of his people, of Jerusalem, but instead of resorting to typical masculine behavior such as ranting and railing, or drafting an oration, or marshaling a political or military response, Jesus was simply moved to tears. He wept.

Sometimes falling to pieces is the only way to put our male psyches back together again. Would that more men spent time every morning, every mid-day, and every evening weeping, knowing that "blessed are they who mourn, for they shall be comforted."

Americans, men in particular, are notorious for trying to tough things out. Our male predicament is that we do too little weeping for our own good. We stuff our souls. The cost is often great, and as one physician aptly states: "Sorrows that find no vent in tears may soon make other organs weep."

Brothers, the future of the very cosmos itself is parched for want of our inner water.

Shedding

And when the day arrives for the last leaving of all,
And the ship that never returns to port is ready to go,

> You'll find me on board, light, with few belongings,
> Almost naked like the children of the sea.

> —Antonio Machado

Too many men live with material clutter that needs to be passed on, dumped, at least sorted out. Elders willingly summon assistance to execute this arduous, oft-agonizing process. They call for help.

Men have found it useful to talk out loud in the trustworthy environs of their support groups about pruning objects and sorting through memories. This serves as a dress rehearsal. Obviously, I'm not referring to jointly owned relics but rather an elder's own personal stuff.

Here's a suggested way to start sorting and shedding. Walk around your house alone. Take your time. Bask in the memories. It may take months or longer before you're sufficiently confident to keep something, pass it on to family or friends, give it to rummage, or take it to the trash. There will always be some private belongings remaining for the bereaved to comb through after we die, but they should be kept to a manageable minimum. Remember, the mission of mature eldering is to bless, not burden, others, including our loved ones.

Shedding unnecessary, outgrown items now not only frees our descendants but also empowers us to live more fully the continuing days with which we're graced. As I was completing my full-time ministry, I undertook a radical pruning program: divesting myself roughly of 80% of my books, 60% of my files, and 40% of my collectibles.

I did this for several reasons. First, I chose to travel more lightly in my final innings. Second, I enjoyed placing professional stuff directly into the hands of up-and-coming colleagues who might appreciate and relish using it. Third, the process blessed me with energy to be fully awake in my present rather than poking around in my past. Of course, I made mistakes; there are possessions I probably should have kept. But so it goes; that's the reasonable gamble of shedding.

And, men, there's more. This shedding process includes pruning lost dreams and futile emotions as well.

It's never too late to release regrets, to forgive and be forgiven. It took 25 years before Michelangelo could forgive a rival for deliberately defacing a set of his drawings. The cruelty associated with that act of vandalism drove Michelangelo into a lengthy depression. By the time he was finally able to forgive, the man who had committed the act was already dead. But Michelangelo still forgave him.

Shedding enables elders proactively to take spiritual stock of our lives, which, after all, is the endpoint of the earthly sojourn. The sage's goal is to keep on living, as unencumbered as possible, amidst the imponderables: What remains for me to be and do? Whom am I summoned to bless? Whose blessing do I still seek? In what ways can I find and deliver joy from here on out?

In men's retreats, early on during the weekend, I invite men to remember a half-dozen men (no small feat for many)—three within the family and three beyond—living or dead, older and younger men, peers too . . . in short, men who've had a telling impact on their life. They're free to mention more, but at least six. Furthermore, I urge the brothers to remember these men in their totality, with regard to both positive and negative influences.

This poses a challenging endeavor, since most men recall more easily the impact of women than men upon their lives. Yet when we fail to "re-member" men, they're ostensibly lost, buried in our consciousness, no longer valued. Our already fragile brothering communion is willfully dismembered.

At the end of the men's retreat I ask my brothers to write a short epitaph or obituary notice (50 words or less) that captures the heart of who they've been, what they've stood for, and how they wish to be remembered as men. Then, as they're comfortable, I invite them to read their portrayal out loud to the other brothers in the circle. They take their self-tribute home, refine and revisit it periodically, as a reminder of how they currently perceive themselves and how they desire to be recalled. This text furnishes a marvelous guidepost, not hitching post, for their evolving elderhood.

Surrendering

> Growing into eldership is spiritual work and requires loosening our grip without losing our grip!
>
> —Terry Jones

Elders, in readying ourselves to be blessed, need to venture beyond the comfortable and familiar into foreign territories of surrender. Poets know this: "Love is plunging into darkness toward a place that may exist" (Marge Piercy), and "love's function is to fabricate unknown-ness" (e. e. cummings).

Surrendering furnishes a most difficult process for high-control, tight-fisted, hyper-knowing men to undergo. It requires emptying. The trick is to give ourselves *over* to another person or principle or place or reality without giving ourselves *away*. Elders recognize that healthy surrender is a final form of being blessed.

Surrendering means letting ourselves be who we truly are at any given age, rather than clinging to what we used to be or might have been. It means permitting ourselves to slow down, just be our age, as fully as possible.

It entails bowing: surrendering to the needs and purposes of the universe, of the community, and finally of ourselves. Bowing daily to all that arises in our journey, dropping our heads in gratitude and acceptance, enables men to get off those high horses we canter around on in life.

It's told of the philosophical giant Krishnamurti that when he was quite old and very frail, he was addressing a large assembly with his customary engaging gentleness. Krishnamurti recognized a questioner and slowly, indeed haltingly, tried to respond to the man in the audience. But he was unsuccessful in mounting a dialogue, so he abruptly stopped, and with poignant vulnerability, conceded that he wasn't mentally sharp anymore, so would the questioner please come down to the front and hold his hand for a moment. What a beautiful example of deep wisdom, of healthy surrender!

The Hindu way of religion emphasizes three pathways to communion with Brahman: the way of knowledge, the way of devotion, and the way of action. Each has its own merits. Surrendering emphasizes the way of devotion: love and affectional bonding. It reminds us that seeking understandably culminates in some form of surrender, and that religion, as is most certainly the case with Unitarian Universalism, is based on relationality and requires ample heartfulness.

We men exhibit moments of maturity, of genuine surrendering, when in recovery programs we turn ourselves over to an Inner or Higher Power. Or when we confess our deepest aches and burdens before our partner or children. As Michael Meade reminds us: "When men start taking about the wounds they carry—their failures, their losses—then we're into something completely different: the slow workings of the soul." Yes, as the old hymn reports, there are times when we supposedly secure, powerful men are "standing in the need of prayer"—standing in the need of help, of divine assistance.

In surrendering to other men, to women, to children, to animals, to God, Spirit of Life, the Holy One, Creative Interchange (call it what we will), submission is not required, but trust is. Indeed, the Hebrew word for faith, *bitachon*, really means trust. Surrender is about forging a vow, pledging our troth, offering and keeping our trust. And surrender means that sacrifices will lie in store for us. For whenever men enter a holy union with either human or divine beings, we don't emerge the same. We are forever changed. We are saved.

Not long before D. H. Lawrence died, he wrote a poem entitled "Shadows," the last refrain of which poetically catches the way I would invite myself, and other brothers, to complete our eldering path:

> And if, in the changing phases of man's life
> I fall in sickness and in misery
> my wrists seem broken and my heart seems dead
> and strength is gone, and my life
> is only the leavings of a life:
>
> and still, among it all snatches of lively oblivion
> and snatches of renewal

odd, wintry flowers upon the withered stem,
yet new, strange flowers
such as my life has not brought forth before, new blossoms of me—

then I must know that still
I am in the hands of the unknown God,
he is breaking me down to his new oblivion
to send me forth on a new morning, a new man.

Lawrence poignantly pinpoints the ultimate brothering act.

I complete my journey in utter trust: surrendering myself back into "the hands of the unknown God," who ushered me graciously into being, nudged and caressed me along this wondrously mysterious path, and "is breaking me down into his new oblivion / to send me forth on a new morning, a new man."

Such is my prayerful hope for brothers everywhere.

Mail Order Information:

For additional copies of *Save the Males*, send $14.95 per book, plus $2 for shipping and handling (CA residents, add 7.75% sales tax). Make checks payable to:

Tom Owen-Towle
3303 Second Avenue
San Diego, CA 92103

Telephone: (619) 295-7067
E-mail: UUTom@cox.net

Printed in the United States
121302LV00004B/213/A